The Power

A Six Part Guide to Self Knowledge

Philip Harland

Wayfinder Press
London, England

Copyright © 2009-2012 Philip Harland
All rights reserved

ISBN-13: 978-0-9561607-0-6
ISBN-10: 0956160700

Know thyself

CONTENTS

For David Grove

1950-2008

Six nights after its birth the chosen child of the Maori is immersed in a stream and hears the Karakia, the formula of words with power that opens its mind to the world for the first time. Then six red stones are taken by the mother and placed in the earth in a sacred place. And those stones join the six of the last generation, and the six that went before, and all the others put there through time.

During its first six days and six nights, the spirit of the baby is kept safe by twelve companions who travel with it. Twelve is the number of stars we try to reach and touch during our journey through life. Twelve and multiples of twelve are the numbers for the trails of the sea, the land, the mind and the spirit.

Those born on the bright moon come into the world when all doors are open to the thirty-six houses in the heavens. Their winds fill with the light of the Universe and open to trails reaching out to the stars.

From Song of Waitaha

The Polynesians used to say that you could tell a Wayfinder by his bloodshot eyes. For much of the voyage he had to stay awake, continually using his highly developed powers of memory and mental calculation to plot the Waka's route. David Grove, who had part Maori, part European ancestry, was staying with me in London towards the end of 2006 and working as usual into the night. One morning he came down to breakfast, eyes only slightly bloodshot, and wondered in that deceptively gentle way of his if I would spend some time with him on his latest work in Emergent Knowledge and the Power of Six, and oh, by the way, write a book on it. I said no way, David, I'm far too busy writing about all the earlier work in Clean Language and Metaphor.

Three weeks later we were sharing a mountain top in North Island, New Zealand, surrounded by electric blue *Agapanthus*, planning the book in some detail, running a therapeutic clinic in Auckland for case history material, and going for long evening walks. It was an intense and productive time. Then I went on to Melbourne to stay with my son and start writing, and David flew off to Missouri, Paris, and Liverpool to take more seminars and salons. Back in London, I ran the Power of Six with my clients, David emailed way-out ideas now and again, I sent him chapters at intervals, and in October 2007 we got together in France to go over an early draft. It was the last time I saw him. He died suddenly in the United States in January 2008.

David Grove created what I believe to be the most innovative work in psychotherapy since Sigmund Freud and made the most fruitful use of therapeutic metaphor since Carl Jung. His presence is on every page of this book, which is dedicated to his extraordinary, deep, and unshakeable devotion to his clients; to his delight in *jeux de mots* and the puns, quips, and carriwitchets of language; to his endless enthusiasm for innovation and experiment; and to his countless little surprises, challenges, and kindnesses. David died young, but he had always been ahead of his time. And it is possible that having developed not one, but six ground-breaking therapeutic methodologies, he felt he had achieved enough for six lifetimes and could now allow whatever would emerge from their interaction and iteration to emerge as it would.

Acknowledgements

Special thanks to James Lawley and Penny Tompkins, neurolinguistic psychotherapists, master trainers of Clean Language, and developers of Symbolic Modeling, for being such a prime resource. For hosting our early research days with David in London; for reading every word of this book in draft; and for their exceptional combination of integrity, humanity, and skill in giving encouragement while offering real improvements.

Carol Thompson, therapeutic counselor and inner clown facilitator. Richard Brenchley, architect and ally. Jennifer de Gandt for her exceptional seminars in Normandy and salons in Paris. Maurice Brasher for his bilingual word play and profound work on etymology, epistemology, and emergence. David's former partner Cei Davies Linn for her determination to keep his legacy alive without compromise. Dr. John Martin for his insights and suggestions. Silvie de Clerck, Anna Piesckiewicz, Noémie Dehouck, Monika Thiel, Lynn Bullock, Lynne Burney, Laetitia Mazauric-Cleyet, Myriam Mora, Patrick Lynch, Dr. Vishwamohan Thakur and Professor Roelof Oldeman for their participation and support. Members of the London Clean and Emergent Research Group for their input to some of the exercises in Part Six, and for being such a reliable and enjoyable resource over the years.

Thanks also to those colleagues around the world who were a part of the development of Emergent Self Knowledge and Sixness through discussion, suggestion, encouragement, and practice. David would want me to acknowledge Dafanie Goldsmith and Dr. Helen Gardyne in New Zealand; Caitlin Walker and Carol Wilson in Britain; Rob and Brenda McGavock, Steven and Karen Briggs in the States; and his mentor, the late Bill Rawlins, linguist, sociologist, and polymath – "The first," David would say, "to analyze what I was doing and to point out that it was made up of six things."

And not least a huge appreciation to all the Power of Six clients who contributed their knowledge of themselves.

Front cover photo: the six-petalled, self-seeding *Agapanthus* (literally, 'love flower') is said to have both magical and medicinal properties. It lines the path to Dafanie Goldsmith's retreat on North Island, New Zealand, where the first seeds of this book were sown.

Notes to the Reader

1 In the text I shall address "you" in your role as either navigator/ facilitator or explorer/client. The context will indicate which of these I imagine you to be in at any one time. If you are a facilitator who has never been a client or a client who has never been a facilitator, by the way, you should put that right immediately. You will be doubly blessed.

2   Rather than use 's/he' or 'his/hers' etc. when referring to gender-unspecified persons, I prefer the traditional singular sense of "they" and "their" (as in "ask a friend if they can help," "each to their own," etc.). And rather than 'himself or herself,' the old gender-neutral 'themself' that is making a comeback (as in "helping someone to help themself" or "asking the client themself").

3 American English spelling is used throughout.

4 All client quotations are real and as near as possible verbatim. Some clients have allowed me to use their real names. I have respected the anonymity of those who wished not to be identified.

5 The information is arranged with two kinds of reader in mind. Those who wish to use the book as a reference can mix and match the parts as they wish. Those who prefer their information to emerge gradually are recommended to follow the structure as it is. My aim is to prepare your thinking and to help you step outside any mindset you might once have had about the way therapy, counseling, or coaching *should* be done – not to change your mind, but to open up your choices. This book is not just about a formula, but a whole new way of thinking about change.

The INTRODUCTION is a quick historical trip into how the Power of Six came about, how I came to be involved, and how it differs from conventional therapies and models of coaching.

PART ONE (*The Powers of Six*) begins with a weekend in Paris and an example of the process in action. It goes on to introduce the underlying principles; discusses how the roles of facilitator and client interact; describes how new information emerges from their interaction; and suggests why the number six is a key constant in the process.

PART TWO (*Knowing the Numbers*) explains the different roles and personalities of the numbers that are at the heart of every Power of Six process.

PART THREE (*Knowing the Network*) describes and illustrates the information network the numbers create.

PART FOUR (*Creating the Network*) is a practical chapter; it introduces and illustrates six basic ways of initiating and orchestrating an information network.

PART FIVE (*Six Degrees of Freedom*) examines a number of real-life cases in detail, with a commentary to help you familiarize yourself with the techniques in practice.

PART SIX (*Emerging*) looks at present and future possibilities. It describes and exemplifies applications of the Power of Six and offers additional exercises.

6 At the end is a section with information you can follow up if you wish to go further. I hope that you will. In the References and the Index you will find that first and second names are not inverted. The order is strictly alphabetical (e.g., David Grove comes under D, not G).

Introduction

Meet my six little friends. They can be yours too. David Grove

I was going to call this *A Hitchhiker's Guide to the Universe of Six*. I had thumbed a ride with a pioneering genius and expected him to do most of the driving. But David Grove's special intelligence was to give what he knew for others to pass on, and that is what this book is about. I offer you an unusual journey, powered by Grove, piloted by me, in which the vehicle, the energy, and the direction will be, I trust, entirely yours.

Why should you read this book? Because words can have an effect on the brain every bit as powerful as drugs, and if you want to use language to help people without the risk of harm to them you will find much that is new here. In the process, you will learn a great deal about the psychology and the step-by-step *practicality* of change. If you are a coach, consultant, counselor, health professional, psychologist, teacher, therapist, or trainer, you will learn how to progress your clients more easily and safely. They will work through their traumas without being retraumatized. They will find a path through the woods of their confusion very quickly indeed and at the end of the day, importantly and properly, they will own their own process. They will heal themselves. As a result, you will find your work less taxing. You will end the day in a more relaxed state, because you will not have been, to quote a psychoanalyst colleague, "stuck in transference all day."

Transference is the redirection onto another person of emotions unconsciously retained from childhood. The term is usually applied to a patient's redirection onto the therapist, but it happens the other way round too. It can be distracting and de-energizing for both parties. The process described in this book considerably reduces transference and so-called counter-transference, because it concentrates the attention of both parties on the client's relationship with their information and not on their relationship with the therapist or coach. As facilitator of this process, you will guide your client through the content of their problem to its structure and beyond its structure to its solution. And you will have had the help of a set of simple but powerful questions. "Six little friends," Grove called them. The numbers will have done most of the work for you.

What qualifies me to be your guide? Before becoming a psychotherapist, I studied architecture and military law, and worked in theater, film, and television. Not an obvious path, you might think, but it brought three things together for me. Learning about building taught me that anything of enduring value could only be constructed from the ground up – by attending first and last to the user's needs rather than to the designer's. As a prosecuting and defending officer in courts martial during military service, I learned both the manipulative and the healing power of words. Language could imprison people, but it could also free them. And from writing and directing drama and documentary, I learned the importance of beginnings and endings, and what happens in-between. The start of any dramatic work – film, play, court case, therapeutic process – is vital in setting up the legitimacy of what happens next. The middle bits have to maintain momentum and help the protagonist surmount obstacles to progress. And the ending – the learning, the resolution – though it may be unexpected, even surprising, has to be true to all that went before.

It was not until I decided that real lives were more interesting than fiction, and realized that human feelings and problems, like cathedrals, cottages, court cases and films, had *a structure,* that I thought about becoming a psychotherapist. I wanted to rewrite the endless conflicts of human existence. Although a part of me believed that we were doing the best we could with what we had, another part told me that most of us could do better.

First I had to find out what it means to be a client, however, because I didn't know myself well enough to be the slightest use to others. Like most people who come from dysfunctional families, I found myself repeating erratic patterns that I couldn't for the life of me understand and was having difficulty sorting out on my own. I went into three years of Jungian analysis and then trained in analytic, humanistic, and cognitive-behavioral models of therapy. But none of these ways of doing therapy left me wanting to be a therapist. They were – are – without exception, *interpretive*. They translate the meaning of a client's experience into metaphors of their own and then attempt to rewrite the original to fit the translation. At best, this is done openly, with the client's consent, but for the most part, it's done unthinkingly and at worst surreptitiously. The balance of power is skewed hugely in favor of the therapist as the prime source of knowledge and authority, and this seemed to me politically, pragmatically, and morally wrong.

Then I came across Neuro-Linguistic Programming (NLP), and an approach to human communication and change that derived from actual experience rather than from generalized theory. NLP had a methodology that was founded, ah yes, on how we *construct* our subjective perceptions. When feelings were messy, as they often were, and the going got rough, as it frequently did, structure was something I could hold on to, like the handrails on a cross-Channel ferry. I qualified as a Master Practitioner, but still found myself having to hallucinate what my clients required in order to solve what I presumed to be their problems. That didn't feel right. I didn't know best. No therapist does. Clients know best. But clients don't always know how to sort and retrieve the knowledge they need. Where is the key to this subliminal store? How can people be facilitated to find it themselves?

In 1995, synchronicity brought me to an experimental workshop in 'Clean Language' run by James Lawley and Penny Tompkins, who had just begun to apply their NLP modeling skills to the work of a peripatetic therapist by the name of David Grove. Here at last were non-interpretive principles that mirrored my own, a methodology that was congruent and reproducible, and a straightforward non-doctrinaire approach to working with people. No external certification was required to practise it. The philosophy of Clean was its own just cause.

Traditional therapies have always centered on the relationship between therapist and client: explicitly in the case of 'client centered' and 'humanistic' approaches, and implicitly in the case of psychoanalysis and its heirs and successors. Actually, analytic models seem to me particularly relationship-centered, drawing attention as they do to feelings of attraction, rage, hatred, dependency and so on that the patient may have towards the therapist, and *vice versa*. Interpreting and confronting these requires the parties to communicate in a workaday language that presumes too much and opens up too many gaps in understanding between them. Clients can be in therapy for years and only the relatively well off can afford it. Meanwhile, health professionals are obliged to treat their patients' psychological problems as behavioral or chemical deficits, and to manage their symptoms with short-lived cognitive techniques or unpredictably mind-modulating drugs. As a result, the underlying patterns that hold problems in place remain largely unresolved and patients find themselves back on a waiting list when the symptoms return – as they often, even usually, do.

Grovian therapies reduce the client's dependency on the therapist considerably. There is a division of labor between facilitator and respondent that echoes the Socratic alliance. But whereas Socrates emphasized his pupils' relationship with what he liked to call the truth, Grove drew his clients' attention to their relationship with themselves. Socrates would take a leading role in deconstructing his pupils' false reasoning before allowing them to share the initiative in a reconstructive second phase. The Grovian way facilitates the client to take responsibility for both. In one of Plato's dialogues, *The Theaetetus*, Socrates describes himself as a midwife on remarkably similar lines to the way Grove would two millennia later. Indeed, says Socrates:

> so far like the midwife that I cannot myself give birth to wisdom ... and though I question others I can myself bring nothing to light, because there is no wisdom in me. The many admirable truths my respondents bring to birth have been discovered by themselves from within.

'Mid' is an Old English preposition whose meaning was 'with'. The role of a good midwife is to be with the mother during pregnancy and childbirth, not directing her. Both Socrates and Grove professed to accompany rather than lead their respondents' gestation and delivery, but the precise, procedural model of questioning that Grove was developing in the nineteen-eighties and nineties, Clean Language, encouraged clients to take by far the greater share of the labor. Clean Language speaks to the intuitive visual, auditory, and kinesthetic metaphors that people use to describe their problems – "dark cloud", "cry from the heart," "knot in the stomach" and so on. When these are treated as coded messages from the unconscious and questioned without interpretation or interference, the client is invariably led to a hurt, imprisoned, or abused 'inner child', and further back yet to an earlier, joyful, pristine state. A remedial or healing resource is sought in the earlier cosmology and brought forward to clear up the present-day problem. Years of therapy are reduced to months, months to weeks.

Grove, Tompkins, and Lawley ran their first joint trainings in Clean Language and Therapeutic Metaphor in Britain in 1996. A few of us who participated in those were invited to join a development group to try out ideas, expand the model, tease and test the key clean questions. One question in particular came up repeatedly in our research: "Where could a problem state or feeling *come from*?" A client's response to the question would invariably take them to a time past; yet basic physics taught us that time and space were inseparable. Information occupying a slot in time had to have its spatial equivalent. The use of *space as a present resource* emerged. We began to move out of our chairs. It was something Gestalt and Psychodrama therapists had been getting their clients to do for years, but the idea of making space itself a protagonist and obliging the therapist to move too was quite new.

And what happened is that our fixed perceptions of therapy as a dialogue between therapist and client following conversational rules changed rapidly and dramatically. The 'Clean' therapist, counselor, coach, etc., became a *facilitator*, freeing the client to seek out physical positions equating to mental spaces containing what had previously been inaccessible or intractable information. The technology that came to be known as 'Clean Space' evolved alongside Clean Language. Space was no longer empty area. It had properties and particularities of its own. Physical space became psychoactive and therapy took on a new dimension.

The concept of 'emergence' was re-emerging as a science in its own right at that time. Systems theorist Jeffrey Goldstein defined emergence as "the arising of novel and coherent structures, patterns, and properties during the process of self-organization in complex systems." In a 1997 article, *Symbolic Modeling: an Overview*, Lawley and Tompkins wrote:

> According to 'self organizing systems theory,' at a certain level of complexity, a system will naturally reorganize … and it is through a heightened awareness of our own patterns that new levels of complexity can emerge. In other words, the system starts to self- correct.

They might equally have said, 'The client starts to do their own therapy.' Grove began to ask if the therapist could be eased even further out of the equation. He suggested that the information-rich spaces clients discovered in a Clean Space procedure would *network together* and that from their self-organization *new knowledge would emerge*. From there it was a small step, though now it seems more like a quantum leap, to applying the iterative principles of the science of emergence to heal the systems of the mind. In the Emergent Self Knowledge process of the Power of Six, the repetition of a single question drives an algorithm of change that prompts a restructuring of the client's personal worldview in which the old stuff – fear, shame, guilt, and so on – reorganizes into a more manageable form and in some cases ceases to exist altogether.

These are exciting times and spaces. *The Power of Six* is your guide to this universe of the self. It introduces a recipe, a prescription, a formula so simple that even I can follow it. My intention is not just that you should get to know this formula, but that you should get into the frame of mind of someone who uses it to do new things. No formula was ever the last word on a subject. $E=mc^2$ doesn't tell the whole story about mass-energy equivalence and the nature of reality. To understand the formulaic procedures for furthering self-knowledge and self-reorganization that you will find in these pages, you do not have to have the slightest grounding in physics or math, I promise, but if I have been convinced of anything while researching this book, against all my schoolboy prejudices, it is that mathematics, pure and applied, determine and condition the cosmos and everything in it, including you and me. In that spirit, I urge you to embrace the numbers. Six new friends will be your companions – sometimes amicable and sometimes awkward, as friends can be – on an extraordinary journey.

§

Part One

THE POWERS OF SIX

You know more than you think you know.
Dr. Benjamin Spock

Part One The Powers of Six

Chapter 1
The Paris Salon

Here we are in the center of the city on a sunny day in September, taking the gilt-mirrored lift to a sixth floor apartment with views over the roofs of one of Baron von Haussmann's elegant *fin-de-siècle* boulevards. David Grove is to present his latest findings in Emergent Knowledge and the Power of Six at one of Jennifer de Gandt's Clean Language salons and I am to make notes for this book. The principles and processes of the new work are a logical development of Clean Language and Clean Space, and at the same time, a preposterous, unquantifiable leap further. "If at first the idea is not absurd," said Einstein, "then there is no hope for it." The Power of Six fulfills this requirement perfectly, which is one of the things that appeals to me about it.

Today we are privileged to meet six accomplished, engaging women: Noémie, Lynn, Laetitia, Monika, Anna, and Thérèse: business coach, movement therapist, information manager, consultant, executive, and marine biologist. One or two are in their 30s, the others in their 40s and 50s. They are French, English, Polish, and German. Curious, alert, and wondering what they have let themselves in for.

Rather than give a dissertation or work one-to-one, David invites the group to embark on a process together. (You will find examples of working one-to-one in the chapters that follow; the questions vary slightly, but the principles are the same.) He asks participants first to:

> *Choose the size of paper you would like.*
> *Find a space in which you would like to work.*
> *Write down or draw something you would like to work on.*

There is a genial buzz of conversation as the women select paper and pens, move around the room, compare notes, continue conversations they had started earlier. Monika finds herself sitting upright at a table, a little formally. Noémie, quiet and polite, is seated on a sofa. Lynn, who smiles throughout, has made herself comfortable on the floor surrounded by cushions. What each of them has done is to select a place and position intuitively related to something that is going on for them currently that they *would like to change*. David's first question refers to what they have written or drawn:

> *What else could go on there?*

A silence descends. It's an unusual question. People think. Write. Laetitia does a little drawing of a figure peeping out from behind a large question mark.

What else could go on there?

The second question is equally unexpected. It is virtually the same:

> *And what else could go on there?*

Everyone adds something to what they have written or drawn. The only voice heard now is David's, every few moments, quietly asking the same question in that soft but assertive, atlanticized antipodean voice of his. A third time:

> *And what else could go on there?*

That initial *"And ..."* has several effects. It induces a mild trance state that keeps distraction at bay and helps clients concentrate on what is going on for them internally. It creates a familiar momentum that encourages information to appear in an atmosphere of safety and security. And it maintains the rhetorical expectation that something can always be added to what has already been expressed.

A fourth question: the same:

And what else could go on there?

A fifth and sixth. After the sixth, the question changes:

And now *what does that statement or drawing know?*

A question that elicits not simply what the statement or drawing knows, of course, but what the person who made it has learned about themself. Some people think the exercise is over. In fact, it has only just begun. Another question sets up a second round:

Is there another place or position that would like you to go to it?

While we were working in Britain and New Zealand earlier in the year, we would be inviting clients to "find another space" or enquire if there was "another place you would like to go." Since working in France and playing with translations (*"Y a-t-il un autre espace où vous souhaitez aller?"*), two things have happened. David has realized that a client's sense of space can be more subtle – a change of position may be as telling as a wholesale move – and he has noticed that the time spent finding the right space can be considerably reduced if the space is encouraged to choose the client rather than the other way round.

Moving to a new space draws the client out of their present entanglement with the problem, just as inviting them to put the problem onto paper does. In order to respond, the client is obliged to project themself mentally into a space that cannot then help but be, or quickly become, 'psychoactive'. It holds information with the potential for inducing subtle changes in brain chemistry and profound effects on perception, awareness, and behavior.

In response to the question, Laetitia stays where she is; Noémie gets up from the sofa and goes to a window; Thérèse, looking uncomfortable, moves nearer the door; Lynn and Anna stay where they are, but position themselves differently. A space is the right space when the client becomes aware of a difference, often small, always significant, in their subjective experience as they move.

People speak of being "drawn" to a corner, to a shaft of light, a window, a certain chair. They might experience a glimmer of recognition beyond words. Taking a step, making a turn, nudging themselves a few centimeters one way or another, can make all the difference. Suddenly the internal world is at one with the external world. When everyone has settled, David asks the same question:

> *And what else could go on there?*

Again, this is asked six times, with a pause between each. The apartment is unusually quiet now. At the end of the round, there is a moment or two for people to reflect, then an invitation to move again or stay put, then another round of six. We continue like this for three or four hours, though, this being France, there is a decent interval for lunch.

At the end of the sixth and final round, I ask participants to share what happened for them. Is there a difference between what they knew at the start and what they know now?

LAETITIA – graceful, informal, seemingly at ease with herself – surprises me by talking about an allergic reaction to certain foods that has affected her life quite badly:

> I was very factual in what I wrote to begin with – about how the doctors keep on saying the next time I collapse my heart might not recover, which is dangerous and quite scary ... and the last thing I wrote is that I can do something about it. This is a signal that something is going wrong. I have to listen to the signal. Food is just the clothes it wears. I learned that my allergy is a kind of denial. I deny it, and just collapse. So it has to do with questions to myself. It leads to *knowing about myself.* Basically, I have the choice now. And *I know I have the choice.*

The italics are mine. They highlight what happens in an Emergent Knowledge process. No surprises here: new knowledge emerges. I believe that at some level we already have this information and the Power of Six allows us to rediscover it. Grove liked to call it "a re-cognization" by the client. More about this anon.

NOÉMIE has been looking at difficult issues she has with her son around the subject of homework. Noémie is a serene 51-year old business coach who speaks evenly and softly, but now there is color and surprise in her voice. I ask her about the difference between her response to the first question and her response to the last.

> The difference at the end was extraordinary, extraordinary! My first statement was on the lines of being a bad mother. I wrote pages full of things that I would like to give my son, but couldn't. And by the sixth, I knew that sometimes I make mistakes, but so what? I can find another space to be in. There are loads of spaces. Here I am by the window. C'est ma place, *et je sais que c'est possible.* This is my place, *and I know it's possible.*

A few months later, Noémie tells me that the situation at home has changed. Whenever the issue of homework comes up, she moves to 'her place.'

> It is the space where I am myself. In this space, I can be centered on the son I love and desire to help.

The move enables her to see her son and his homework in a different light. It is not a dramatic move, but the effect is considerable.

> It's a very different sensation for me. In the other space, I was playing someone else's role. I realized it was my mother's! Whenever she tried to explain anything to me, it created a blockage – is that the word? I relate directly to my son now and not to the homework. I can marvel at him. And what used to be hell has become very bearable and sometimes even enjoyable.

Noémie goes on to describe how she has carried this learning into her corporate coaching, enabling clients to clear emotional blocks in their lives and at work by the simple six-step expedient of finding the right psychic space.

MONIKA volunteers. She tells us about a back problem she has been suffering since a climbing accident fifteen years ago. Monika is a 40-year old management consultant with a warm demeanor that belies the discomfort and pain she feels in most of the time. I realize now why she has been sitting upright for most of the day. What does she know now, compared to what she knew at the start? Her response is measured, but clearly there are deep-seated feelings involved:

> The statement I wrote to begin with was very much linked to getting rid of the pain in my back. I found myself focused on past experiences linked to getting rid of the sadness around my parents' divorce and my role in the family from early childhood, that of a mediator.

Monika was brought up in the Bavarian Alps near the Austrian border. She was an only child who adored her father, a musician, painter, mountaineer, and storyteller. They shared dreams, played, and went climbing together. Life at home was not so idyllic, however. The relationship between her parents was tense and Monika found herself taking her father's side:

> Somehow, he seemed misunderstood by my mother. And yet I had to understand one day that my dad was not all that wonderful. My father left my mother and me in order to live with another woman. And it turned out that he had intended to do so during many years prior, when he lived both relationships in parallel. All those years seemed suddenly like a lie. All the time I was mediating, defending him, seemed wrong.

At the age of twenty, Monika left Germany to study in England and distance herself from the role she had taken at home. Five years later, she moved to France, but what she calls "the constant shadow of an untreated past" followed her. She began psychotherapy. And six months later, she went climbing again. There was an accident. She fell and fractured one of her lower vertebrae.

> Needless to say, my feelings of pain did not pass after physical therapy. I came to believe that this accident was a rather heavy attempt to rid myself of old memories of the influence of my father. He came to see me as I lay in bed. For the first time, I told him everything and that I would never forgive him. But in twelve more years of psychotherapy, I started to understand his importance in my life – everything that I started off, all my values and beliefs, were influenced by him.

Monika decided that it was time to stop recycling the past and to look ahead, and today she has been using the process to support and reinforce her decision. And what Monika knows now has nothing to do with the pain. It is about enjoying every moment of her life.

> Towards the end of David's questioning, I suddenly found myself walking away from the past. I was no longer focusing on the pain, I was experiencing fully the present. And now it is about smelling flowers, observing things, using all my senses. It's very beautiful. I have the confidence that it will happen the way it is supposed to happen, and *I know now that it's all within me,* this connection with *the inner being that knows.*

I have heard many stories about the ways new knowing emerges during these sessions. I have seen the way existing, often deeply hidden, information is transformed into knowledge, and knowledge into resolution and healing. That can happen in any therapy, given time. It is unusual here in that it can happen so quickly. And also, and not least, because it is *self-organizing.* The procedures of the Power of Six encourage – indeed, practically oblige – the self to reorganize itself, and as a result the client gets to own every jot and scintilla of their own process.

What needs to be in place for that to happen?

§

Part One The Powers of Six

Chapter 2
The Principles Self-healing
Information
Necessary conditions

First, a note on the Grovian philosophy of self-healing in the context of Emergent Self Knowledge, followed by an explanation of what information is in this context; and then a summary of the information-based principles of self-healing from which the Powers of Six are derived.

Self-healing

Throughout our lives, we encounter problems that we find hard to understand or resolve. We create these problems in ways that are uniquely structured to our personalities, which means that the solutions have to arise from the same uniqueness. We achieve this by tapping into the inner worlds of our own wisdom, those immeasurable reservoirs of information that maintain us as individuals and to which no one else – no partner, teacher, counselor, or healer – has access. The Power of Six supports us to retrieve the specific information we need to resolve our problems in a process of self-discovery that leads to self-reorganization.

Information

The 'information' we are talking about here is not made up of facts acquired by study or instruction, but is, literally, in-formation, that which is formed from within: properties and patterns in the form of memories, metaphors, images, snippets, thoughts and sensations that are processed and evaluated by the brain to influence the formation and transformation of other properties and patterns.

Information is thus *potential knowledge*. It is what emergence researcher Maurice Brasher calls "a candidate for knowledge." It becomes knowledge when we recognize it, ascribe primacy to it, give it significance, order, meaning, a name.

Information, like energy, does real work. It changes brain chemistry and neuronal activity, it changes behavior, and it changes lives. Systems thinker Gregory Bateson identified it as "the difference that makes a difference." There is no need for the conscious mind to perceive, much less appreciate, how this difference happens. It is our inner intelligence at work.

Necessary conditions

The Power of Six is a methodology for eliciting and utilizing our inner intelligence. It is driven by six necessary conditions (Fig. 1):

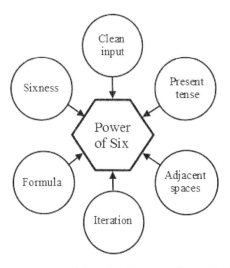

Figure 1. Six necessary conditions for the operation of the Power of Six

1 *Clean Input*. Whether the facilitator asks the Power of Six questions, or clients ask the questions of themselves, the principle is the same: questions are minimally assumptive, non-suggestive, and metaphor-free. They are: "What do you know?" "And what else do you know?" "And now what do you know?"

2 *The Present Tense.* All Power of Six questioning, all client information, knowledge, and experience, whatever time scale it may refer to, is elicited and maintained in the here and now: "What do you know?" "And what else do you know?" "And now what do you know?"

3 *Adjacent Spaces.* The mental and/or physical spaces the client's information occupies have a notional boundary within which the facilitator's questions are addressed. As the problem and its location relative to the client are established (see Part Three), the spaces that define the client's construction of the problem appear. New information is accessed in adjacent spaces.

4 *Iteration.* The Power of Six questions have an iterative effect, each client response feeding back to inform the next. The same thing happens in the networking of spaces and in further rounds of questioning: as information increases and iterates, complexity builds and eventually collapses or reorganizes, allowing self-healing and resolution to emerge.

5 *Formula.* In each round of questioning, the same procedure based on the same questions is repeated. The predictability of the Power of Six de-emphasizes the client/facilitator relationship and encourages clients to discover what they need to know for themselves.

6 *Sixness.* Six numbers drive the process. There are six basic questions to a round, (see the next chapter and Part Two), six parts to an information network (Part Three), and six parts to an action plan (Part Four).

Emergence is the meta-process these principles serve. There is more on emergence in Chapter 5 of Part One, and more about each of the necessary conditions throughout the book. The first two – *Clean Input* and *The Present Tense* – are common to all Clean processes. The next three – *Adjacent Spaces, Iteration,* and *Formula* – are shared with Clean Space and Emergent Knowledge generally. All six conditions are present in the Power of Six. *Sixness* is exclusive to it.

§

Part One The Powers of Six

Chapter 3
The Process

All great things are simple.   Winston Churchill

Philosophically and practically, the Emergent Self Knowledge process of the Power of Six is unlike any formula you may have come across in the fields of psychotherapy and self-development. It consists of a single question and five repeats. That is it, basically. The only approach I know that is remotely comparable has a so-called Enlightened Master encouraging followers to focus on a single question such as "Who am I?" or "What is Life?" for three days on end, a process that asks of its devotees an unusual level of dedication.

Because the Power of Six is such a simple operant, it is able to contain complexity. The numbers at its heart can be said to hold the client's problem, so that client and therapist or coach do not have to. If as facilitator you were questioning your client directly, rather than questioning something they have written or drawn, as in the Paris salon, your opening question might simply be:

What do you know?

There are a couple of minor variants on this, as we shall see. This opening question is followed by:

And what else do you know?

which is repeated four more times:

And what else do you know?
And what else do you know?
And what else do you know?
And what else do you know?

Musicians know how difficult it is to improvise music without a beat. The repetitive patterns of the Power of Six send a message to the higher nervous system that here is a meter, a measure, around which the mind can play safely. This is not the kind of security that written music provides. No-one here tells the performer what to play. The cue from the Power of Six conductor is more on the lines of: "I will look after the beat; this is your time and space; you can now be yourself."

The Emergent Knowledge questions are arguably even 'cleaner' than the original Clean Language questions. They are certainly simpler and easier to remember. The standard Clean Language model has upwards of thirty questions, any one of which could be relevant at any one time, whereas you could close this book now, ask these six self-knowledge questions of anyone, and get some kind of result. Do come back, however. It took an exceptional therapist thirty years of unremitting trial and error to distil everything he knew into something as unfussy as this, and if you would like to find out more about how the process works and about the bigger picture of which the questions are a part, you need to read a little further.

The Power of Six, like Clean Language and Clean Space before it, emerged within the framework of a philosophy dedicated to helping people help themselves *in the way only they could.* These were not intended to be elitist procedures. Grove was adamant that his methods had to be straightforward, teachable, and transferable. They had to be capable of supporting sophisticated therapeutic interventions, but also of combining readily with other disciplines – medicine, teaching, coaching, and so on – and even adapting for conversational use.

Increasingly in my work as a therapist, I find that whatever the client or the condition, the standard patterns of the Power of Six deliver at least as well as more elaborate methods and usually more quickly. Given the many choices of approach available to me, it then becomes more a matter of *my will to be simple.* I shall have more to say on this in the next chapter, 'Facilitator and Client'. Being simple is not always easy.

How did the idea of a standard pattern of questioning take shape? In the nineteen-eighties, when David Grove was developing Clean Language and Therapeutic Metaphor for the symptomatic treatment of trauma, the sequence in which the initial questions were asked was gradually refined by David and his partner Cei into a code that followed a typical and teachable (though not, in practice, invariable) order:

.   *And how do you know when* [e.g. you're feeling very sad]?
        And where is [the feeling as described by the client]?
        And whereabouts is it?
        And does it have a size or a shape?
        And that is like what?

There was no shortage of directions in which the process could go after that, but the first inkling of a formula had appeared. Another formulaic trace appeared in the Grovian practice of Intergenerational Healing, when the search for the origins of a symptom or the source of a redemptive metaphor would take the client back in time:

$$\text{from body} \rightarrow \text{to biography} \rightarrow \text{to ancestry}$$
$$\rightarrow \text{to culture} \rightarrow \text{to land} \rightarrow \text{to cosmology}$$

in a methodical six-stage time trail which led eventually to work in spatial sorting and was later formalized into the basic six-step, and then more sophisticated twelve-step, quasi-formulaic procedures of 'Clean Space'.

The Power of Six abides by the same procedural logic, but takes the systematic principle further. It is a *modus operandi* for seeking solutions at any level of expertise; an algorithm that enables the emergence of new knowledge and healing whatever the client's starting point; a prescription that, if followed to the letter, will engage clients with their symptoms directly and change the neuro-chemistry of the brain in ways that are wholly self-generated.

The neural pathways of learning have been well documented by scientists such as Joseph LeDoux in *The Emotional Brain* and Walter Freeman in *How Brains Make Up Their Minds*. Freeman shows how the strengths of the connections between neurons are continually shaped by each new insight. LeDoux describes the chemical changes that strengthen and stabilize synaptic connections, resulting in what he calls the creation of "extinction-resistant learning" in the brain:

> After conditioning, the response of individual cells to the conditioned stimulus is increased (the same input produces a bigger output). In addition, individual cells develop stronger interconnections, so that when one fires the others also fire.

Applying this critical finding in the context of self-organization, we can say that the procedures of the Power of Six *condition the brain to learn from itself*. This is no ordinary conditioner. It disentangles, improves manageability, and restores shine and vitality to the parts other conditioners cannot reach. The repeated question, "And what else do you know?" is a conditioned stimulus that prompts not just more of the same with each repetition, but a series of enhanced outputs leading the client beyond rethinking and modified feeling to extinction-resistant learning.

"All people by nature desire to know," said Aristotle. Physical or psychological symptoms are not something to be feared, ignored, or evaded. They are signals from the bodymind that it is attempting to heal itself. The Power of Six weaves a formulaic spell over such symptoms. It enables them to proclaim what they know, to reveal their strengths and weaknesses, to tap their reserves, and to achieve their goals – and yet to go further, for that is the nature of emergence. It may be a radically different approach to the medical model and to conventional therapies, but it is entirely compatible with either.

§

Part One The Powers of Six

Chapter 4
Facilitator and Client

Half the words we use have no meaning whatever, and of the other half each man understands each word after the fashion of his own folly.   Joseph Conrad

I ask one thing of you in your role as a Power of Six facilitator: a willingness to give up any preconceptions you might have about guiding the journeys of those you serve. The master navigators of Polynesia who traversed the southern oceans imagined themselves at the still center of the universe and the land they sought as *coming to them* through the benign agency of the changing winds, the ocean swell, and the stars. Your job as a facilitator is to be the still center that engages your clients with their own wisdom.

In these chapters, you will learn a number of ways of asking a single question six times. Temperamentally or philosophically, that will not suit everyone. Some highly qualified professionals will find it difficult to let go the learning they have accumulated or the control they are used to exercising: to allow the client do most of the work and for their own input to be significantly reduced. It may feel like a denial of all those years of study and sacrifice. For others, it will feel like a natural development that permits them to take their expertise to another level. And for some it will be the radical breakthrough that they always believed was possible, but didn't quite know how to achieve.

Evolution, revolution, or a step too far? You will decide for yourself. The role of a Power of Six facilitator has its routines, but is never predictable. You will be as intrigued by your clients' idiosyncrasies as you ever were. You will feel as pleased or as challenged by their progress or lack of it as you would in any other modality. There are fewer choices for you to make, but the timing of your choices is critical. You will learn to wait long enough for the client to absorb the new information that appears as a result of your questioning, but not so long that other things intervene and compromise the internal rhythm of their processing. You will learn to pitch your tone of voice so that it is not too conversational, because that will draw the client's attention away from themself and on to you; and yet so that it is not too remote, because that will have the same effect.

Discipline is a virtue here. Your patience will be tested at times and you will be tempted to revert to your old ways: to agree or disagree with your client, to confirm or contradict their experience, to comfort or confront them, to offer reasoned alternatives, or to introduce your own stories and metaphors in a sleight-of-mouth attempt to show them the true way. Resist such temptations! That master of psychological realism, Joseph Conrad (author of *The Heart of Darkness*, etc.), knew it well: half the words we use mean nothing to other people, and when it comes to the other half they will make meaning of their own.

So batten down the hatches, stick to the linguistic, syntactic, and strategic disciplines you will learn here, honor the numerical imperative and follow the Power of Six procedures exactly – or in some cases a little flexibly, as I shall explain later – and you will always be on course.

In your role as client/explorer, you need make no special provision to embark on this journey. To paraphrase Douglas Adams, you might not go where you intended to go, but you will end up where you needed to be. In the process, you will be told nothing. You will only be asked to *say what you know*. The Power of Six, like Clean Language and Clean Space before it, operates from self-regulating, self-determining principles. It may be facilitator-led, but it is unequivocally client-driven. Your facilitator will not attempt to suggest anything to you, or to persuade you of anything, or to lead you down any hypothetical path, or to interpret, evaluate, or examine anything you say. They will be concerned only with the structural and functional components of your process, not its content. The content – rightly, beyond question – is yours alone. In responding to the question, "What do you know?" in the context of whatever it is that you want or that troubles you, you will be generating a set of information points that will network together to provide the information you need (Figure 2).

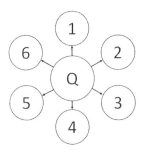

Figure 2. One question drives the information network

The natural connectivity of the network will help you decode your own symptoms and create a context for change. The knowledge that enables you to do this will emerge naturally. It will *come to you*. It cannot be given to you and nor can you go to it directly.

Where should you start? You may have a puzzle you wish to unravel, a goal to pursue, a project to explore, a problem with anxiety or panic attacks, a pain without apparent cause, a communication or relationship issue to resolve, a difficulty with anger, guilt, or forgiveness. Your starting point may be any state, thought, belief, or condition. It may be expressed in a drawing, a sentence, a sigh, or a shrug of the shoulders. These outward representations of your internal state are uniquely yours and so is their resolution. When conventional commonsense or intelligence fail you, the Power of Six is a means of tapping into the reservoirs of your own wisdom. What you find there may mean that your original need dissolves. The distinction you once perceived between yourself and what you wanted may disappear altogether.

"How shall I know what to say?" asked Alice. "Begin at the beginning," the King said gravely, "and go on till you come to the end, then stop." You know more than you think you know. And you will know when you have said what you wanted to say.

§

Part One The Powers of Six

Chapter 5
Emergent Knowledge

The swarm knows more than the sum of what every bee knows.
                                        Kevin M. Passino

Rumor has it that Archimedes' discovery of a formula for calculating volume and density came to him while he was on one of his visits to the local baths. His sudden realization about a body's displacement of water may have come about when he slipped on a bar of soap, but we can be sure that the actual mathematics involved were the result of a great deal of earlier brainwork.

When we add one idea to another, things can get knotty (or slippery) and intricate. Complexity builds over time, then tends to reorganize suddenly, when simple solutions emerge. If you have ever woken in the morning with an idea about something you gave up on the night before, you will have experienced emergence in action. When enough separate but related components are given the time and opportunity to interact, something new happens.

Archimedes legendary cry of "Eureka!", by the way, comes from the same root as 'heuristic', a strategy for working your way towards the solution to a problem. Take the prescribed steps over and over again in an iterative process and you are likely to get the results. Eureka. You can *expect* emergence to occur.

What is an iterative process?

My client COLIN is having trouble trying to communicate with his girlfriend. They are very much involved, but driving each other round the bend, because she is very expressive emotionally and Colin is not. He struggles to recognize his feelings, never mind express them. What Colin wants, as he puts it, is "To know what is inside." If I were to ask him a succession of "What do you know about that?" questions, he would probably not get much further than his first answer ("Nothing"), because my questions, being simply repetitive, would likely produce more of the same. However, if my second question is, "And what *else* do you know about that?" Colin is obliged to find new information that incorporates and allows for his first response. "Nothing" is no longer sufficient.

"And what else?" is an iterative question. Through a succession of these, Colin is able to build on what he knows and to get successively closer to discovering "what is inside." It turns out to be not only a cozy mixture of love and joy, but also a bunch of disagreeable feelings like shame, guilt, and fear. Iterative questioning helps him find out a great deal more about what he had hidden from himself.

What are the differences between iteration, interaction, and integration? And what are their places in the chain of events that lead to emergence (Figure 3)?

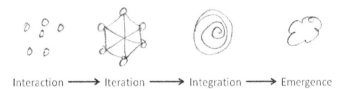

Interaction ⟶ Iteration ⟶ Integration ⟶ Emergence

Figure 3. Nodes of information interact, leading to
iteration, integration, and eventual emergence

Interaction is the lower-level behavior from which a higher-level pattern, integration, emerges, and in the living organisms we are talking about here (you, me, and Colin), it does so via an intermediate process of iteration. Iteration is the repetition of a rule or procedure applied to the result of the previous application, a means of obtaining successively closer approximations to the solution of a problem or of generating something new. As Colin *interacts* with the Power of Six questioning, the information his bodymind generates *iterates* with everything else that he knows, consciously or not, about himself and the world, *integrates* in some very personal way ... and *emerges* as a learning that enables him to improve his relationship with his girlfriend and to enhance his life as a whole.

Colin is thus *enabled*. He *can do*. The word 'can' has the same root as 'know'. They come from a nice Old English verb, 'cnawan', which combined both. *To know is to be able.* Knowledge, as Francis Bacon reminds us, is power.

As recently as the mid-twentieth century, many scientists still believed that knowledge had some kind of independent metaphysical existence. Science philosopher Michael Polanyi went to some lengths to point out that knowledge is in fact personal, constructed of patterns of neural activity within individual brains. As the question, "And what else do you know?" is repeated, the brain is obliged to work further while still making allowance for its earlier answers. It is this cyclical, largely unconscious, 'taking into account' that gives the questions their iterative power.

A tennis player attempts to optimize the serve by taking into account what happened in the earlier serves, what is happening now, and what they wish to happen next. Each bounce of the ball, each shift of the hips, each thought about the importance of the point, are all part of the act of serving as a whole. When enough of these separate but related components interact, iterate, and integrate, an emergent system, the serve, occurs, with properties unlike those of its contributory components.

Life itself is an emergent feature of the history of the planet. Our individual identities derive from a legion of conflicting needs and desires combining so that the perception of a single unified 'self' emerges. Or, rather, continues to emerge. We are in a continual state of emergence, as the self-determining system that is you or I acquires self-knowledge and learns from itself.

Acquiring knowledge is like accumulating capital: it increases at compound interest. In fact, knowledge goes one better, as the 19th century mathematician Charles Babbage pointed out:

> The increase of knowledge produces a more rapid rate of progress, whilst the accumulation of capital leads to a lower rate of interest. Capital thus checks its own accumulation; *knowledge thus accelerates its own advance* [my italics].

What advances is an intelligence with novel but consistent qualities that seemed not to exist before. It is an *embodied* experience, which makes it more of a challenge to unravel than a purely intellectual or material event. Once Grove and I were musing on the felt experience of emergence:

> DG It's as if something is missing which then reappears.

> PH Like the French for "I miss you" is actually, *"Tu me manques,"* literally, "You are missing **in** me."

> DG That's it. The thing that was missing in me has returned. The Maori is *"Aroha noa."* The Aroha noa, the *grace* I lacked has re-emerged. It is now, as the French say, *reconnue,* re-cognized, known again.

The emergence of knowledge has many metaphors. It has been likened to: crossing a threshold
> a bringing to light
> an unfolding
> a blossoming
> a collapse of complexity
> a moment of grace
> an epiphany.

An epiphany is a showing (*phany*) forth (*epi*), a sudden intuitive insight into the essential meaning of something. My client Colin, struggling with acknowledging his feelings and trying to "look inside", has a sudden memory of a little box he owned as a child. He remembers that as a six-year old he had decided to lock his distress at losing his mother into this box. He has been locking away his difficult feelings ever since.

An epiphany is often initiated by some simple, commonplace occurrence, like finding the one piece of the puzzle that makes the picture complete. As a small child, I used to enjoy building things from wooden blocks. To construct a pyramid, I learned to place three blocks in a line, add two, and top it off with one (Figure 4).

Figure 4. A system solution: emergence in action

Six simple operations, but the thrill of positioning the sixth could only be achieved when the first five were in place. At that moment the whole became more than the sum of its parts. This was a system solution: emergence in action.

One of the first to conceive of the *idea* of emergence was the philosopher Plato, who pointed out that the meaning of a word was more than the sum of its individual letters. But it was not until the nineteen-forties that the modern 'discoverer' of emergence, the Latvian-German philosopher Nicolai Hartmann, would declare unequivocally that:

> An emergent property of a system is one that is not a
> property of any component part of that system.

A theme taken up by many scientists and philosophers since. In a 2002 paper, *The Re-Emergence of 'Emergence'* (recommended for an historical and theoretical overview of the subject), complexity researcher Peter A. Corning writes of the evolution of emergent systems in which:

> quantitive, incremental changes can lead to qualitative
> changes that are different from, and irreducible to, their
> parts.

The behavior of every dynamic system arises from the interaction of its parts and cannot be predicted from what we know of the parts in isolation. An ant's nest is a fully emergent system. Ants as individuals are not very bright, at least not by our anthropocentric standards, yet they develop hugely intelligent, self-sustaining communities. In sharing *information*, they generate *intelligence*.

Effective agreement between two or more people does not follow from a recapitulation of their separate positions, but from applying the result of their last discussion to the next discussion until agreement emerges. Single brain cells are largely autonomous, but their interactions form larger entities from which complex functions way beyond the competence of single neurons emerge. A supreme example of emergence is human consciousness, a property of bodymind iterations with very different qualities to its contributory components of sensory processing, electrical signaling, chemical exchange, neural synchrony, etc. – a whole at a higher level of self-organization that is not only unpredictably more than, but also distinctly different to, the sum of its parts.

How do iteration and emergence apply in therapy, coaching, and counseling, where it may only take one or two small changes to produce life-changing effects? Systems theorist Fritjof Capra explains in *The Web of Life* how small differences are amplified into large ones through a process of "self-reinforcing feedback." A small difference feeds into the system → the system performs better → the difference is confirmed → the rewards are reinforced. Here is a simple example: a state of tension can be reduced easily and quickly by taking a deep diaphragmatic breath, which relaxes the body, which makes it less tense, which makes it easier to take more deep diaphragmatic breaths. The effect accelerates its own cause. Just as, say, laughter, an emergent effect of feeling good, releases endorphins, a cause of feeling good, and a good dose of endorphins produces a buoyant feeling that makes us more likely to laugh.

Emergence will not arise if its various parts simply co-exist. They must meet and unite in some way. They must *affect* each other. In the late 1960s, the American biologist Dr. John Bonner Buck made a study of *Photinus pyralis*, a species of fireflies found at night on a tidal river in Thailand. He showed that after a period of interaction, the independent, self-seeking flashing of individual fireflies would gradually synchronize to light up the whole riverbank. I have seen the effect for myself at a smaller scale on the Greek island of Paxos. Buck explained the phenomenon as beginning with nothing more complex than a mating display. A male firefly would flash to attract a female. A female or two would flash back. More flies would be attracted, leading to the emergence of synchronous flashing, which maximized the light output of the whole group, which attracted more fireflies, resulting in more flashing, more mating, and so on. Each small part of the system affected the others until something larger than their totality emerged. Buck called the process "voluntary synchrony".

His finding opened up a new branch of science that resulted in a large number of studies of 'bottom-up' phenomena and the importance accorded to rhythmic neural processes and consistency in what became known as "small-world networks". The term was coined by mathematician Steven Strogatz and sociologist Duncan Watts in a 1998 paper, *Collective Dynamics of Small-World Networks*. They concluded that very few 'weak links' (or 'social bridges,' or 'short cuts') were needed to make a given world small and predicted that small-world architecture would turn out to be prevalent across a wide variety of technical, social, and biological systems.

And so it turned out. In the biological system we know as a human being, the procedures of the Power of Six help create the links and build the bridges between adjacent bits of a person's information so that they interact and affect each other ... to form a small-world network ... whose parts iterate ... resulting in a collective intelligence from which something novel emerges.

Interaction, iteration, and emergence are complex events, but in the context of a therapeutic intervention, we can define the simple behaviors necessary for them to occur as:

> *Repeatedly applying a set of questions that enable the information that ensues from the responses to be added to the result of the previous application until new knowledge emerges or healing takes place.*

Rhythmic (repetitive) neural activity prompted by the persistent application of the same question results in voluntary (self-organizing) synchrony: a harmonization of the simultaneous activity of bodymind components to produce a dynamic, emergent, consistent effect. People get better. They solve their problems. They transform their symptoms. And surprisingly (or not, depending on your point of view) they do it themselves.

In the theater of self-organization, one character has a special part to play.

§

Part One The Powers of Six

Chapter 6
What Is So Special About Six?

If you had told me when I first became a psychotherapist that I would reduce everything I had learned to six questions, I would have invited you to pull the other one. At that time, I hadn't come across Einstein's dictum about absurd ideas.

The number six arose out of Grove's application of network theory to the practice of spatial sorting. (There is more on spatial sorting in Parts Two and Three.) Six is a rule of thumb governing the number of data points necessary for information to reach a critical mass. It has been shown to be pervasive throughout nature, problem solving, and social interaction.

Take the example of a rather large network. In his book, *Just Six Numbers: The Deep Forces That Shape The Universe*, Britain's Astronomer Royal Martin Rees puts forward the view that the entire cosmos is governed by a combination of six mathematical constants. He calls them the ingredients of a recipe for the universe.

> Each of these six plays a crucial and distinctive role ... and together they determine how the universe evolves and what its internal potentialities are.

The six values physicists call 'epsilon', 'lambda', 'omega', 'n', 'd' and 'q' describe the fundamental properties of everything from atoms to life, to clusters of galaxies, to space itself. It seems remarkable that something whose starting point can be specified in just a few numbers can evolve into perhaps the greatest emergent system of all: the bundle of spacetime, matter, and energy we know and love that is the universe. Physicist Paul Davies, in *The Goldilocks Enigma*, describes the six numbers as sitting in a fine-tuned band of values – neither too big nor too small, but just right, like Baby Bear's porridge – outside which life as we know it would be impossible. If any one of the six had been only a little different, we would not exist. The cosmic number 'omega', for example, is a ratio that measures the relative importance of gravity and expansion energy in the universe. Had the ratio been only a little higher, the universe would have collapsed long ago; a little lower and no galaxies would ever have formed.

Coincidence or not (why not five values, or nine?), Davies and others point out that it is the *synthesis* of the six that gives them their significance, in ways that we would not appreciate if we were to consider them one at a time. From the integration of six distinctive values, everything we know has emerged.

It does not take a huge leap of imagination to suppose that a number that describes the cosmos would be found to operate at many different levels within it. If you have ever met a stranger at a party and discovered that you were linked through a surprisingly small number of acquaintances, you will have experienced the power of six at an everyday level. In 1929, in a short story entitled *Chain-Links*, the Hungarian writer Frigyes Karinthy speculated that any two people in the world could be linked through a chain of no more than five acquaintances. Forty years later, social psychologist Stanley Milgram set up a study at Harvard to investigate the anecdotal evidence and concluded that the average length of such a chain was in fact six – remarkably close to Karinthy's prediction.

Milgram's discovery led to a large number of studies to investigate and explain the phenomenon, and to scores of problem-solving techniques based on five, six, and seven steps. Systems and creativity researcher John Martin cites Tudor Rickards' 'Multiple Redefinition' technique, in which a person is taken through six mental modes (Reorienting, Analytic, Motivational, Magical, Metaphorical, and Off-beat), singly and systemically, to generate the solution to a problem. Martin also notes Bernd Rohrbach's 'Six-Step Brainwriting' exercise, in which six people sit round a table, generate three ideas each, and pass them to the next person to develop. When the papers are returned, a total of 108 (6 x 3 x 6) ideas have been generated, of which six are short-listed for developing further. In Part Six, under 'Teams', you will find an imaginative adaptation of this idea that applies the principle of sixness to corporate communications.

In the late seventies, the co-creators of NLP, Bandler and Grinder, came up with the 'Six-Step Reframe,' an exercise designed to turn a perceived problem around in six interdependent stages:

1 Identify the behavior to change
2 Establish communication with the 'part' responsible
3 Identify the positive intention of the part and its behavior
4 Generate alternative ways of satisfying the same intent
5 Ask the part if it will agree to use these new behaviors preferentially
6 Check for any internal conflict regarding the change.

Grove's former partner, Cei Davies, recalls him first making mention of "six degrees of separation" in his tutorials in the late eighties, but it was not until he developed the theory and practice of Intergenerational Healing in the mid-nineties that the number found its first, probably unconscious, expression in his work. The questions he was raising at the time were "From where and when did the client's symptoms originate?" and "Where could a source of healing be found?" The answers were to be revealed in a series of six nodes in spacetime (Figure 5).

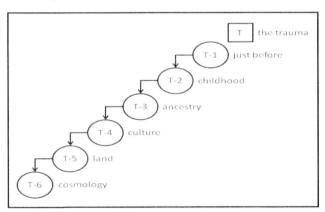

Figure 5. Six sources of information and redemption

In this chain of related events, 'T' represents the worst moment of the defining trauma in a client's life and T minus one ('T-1') a time just before: a moment in which the client's emotional development is typically frozen, obstructed, or takes a divergent path. T minus two ('T-2') holds childhood information that precedes T-1; 'T-3' intergenerational information via parents, grandparents, and great-grandparents; 'T-4' cultural and background information; 'T-5' immigration or land of origin information; and 'T-6' spiritual, religious, or nature of the universe information.

In what Grove characterized as "pulling the client back" from T-1 through T-6, the therapist seeks a client-generated redemptive resource that existed prior to the history of the trauma. The resource is developed and taken forward in time to clear up contributory factors to the trauma en route to healing the symptom.

But why *six* sources of information and redemption? Why *six* steps to 'reframing', 'brainwriting', and 'redefinition'? In 2008, Microsoft researchers Eric Horvitz and Jure Leskovec reported on their study of the largest social network ever analyzed: 30 billion Instant Messenger communications between 240 million people around the world. Their report concluded that the average chain needed to connect IM users was 6.6. "The idea of six degrees of separation goes beyond folklore," they concluded.

That same year in the mayoral elections in London, a political party was inviting its members to email just six other people as a strategy for getting their candidate into City Hall. Did six sound like a decent round number to them – not as mean as five, but less bothersome than seven? Or were they, like Milgram, Rees, Rohrbach, and others, tapping into some deeper design?

The eminent Dutch ecologist Roelof Oldeman points out the parallels between psychological and *biological* growth and development. There is a fundamental six at the heart of the double helix structure of DNA, the self-replicating transmitter of all genetic information: five 'base pairs' – the sixth an 'adjustment zone' – five more base pairs – an adjustment in the sixth – and so on. Six is also fundamental to tree and plant architecture. Professor Oldeman tells me: "We found the same principles emerging from completely different levels of organization of the living."

The six steps he and his colleagues have observed in tree and plant growth are not in a linear order, but "like steps in a dance, each in a different place and time as life and the stresses of life demand."

This is a *system solution*, the intention of every six-step exercise in problem solving, therapy, and creativity. Systems researcher

John McCrone, reviewing Fritjof Capra's book, *The Hidden Connections*, explains the systems view as holistic and organic:

> A mechanical system simply acts according to its instructions. But a living system, with its internal intelligence and complex feedback organization, reacts to the meaning it finds in the information. The system *selects the messages to which it listens and then evolves its own response*. [My italics]

Human beings are a prime example of living systems with internal intelligence and complex feedback responses. Work by Jon Kleinberg at Cornell University shows that as individuals we are very effective at responding to information by finding short, selective paths through our social and information networks. The World Wide Web is an example of a network that enables the construction of very short paths between problem and solution. As a node with only local knowledge of the network (at home in London, England), I was able to reach a node with the global information needed to achieve my desired outcome (booking a flight to Auckland, New Zealand) in only six clicks. At another time, it might have taken me a click more or less. The point is that the number was surprisingly small.

Milgram's and Kleinberg's results demonstrate not only the existence of such short chains of 'adjacencies', but also the ability of people at finding them. We do not always know how we get to where we arrive – we can only take one step at a time – but we get there all the same.

In any self-organizing system, no two elements are ever far apart in spacetime or non-local terms, which means that one part cannot help but affect, and be affected by, the others. In his stage play, *Six Degrees of Separation*, John Guare put it this way:

> Everybody on this planet is separated by only six other people. Six degrees of separation. The President of the United States. A gondolier in Venice. It's a profound thought. How every person is a new door, opening up into other worlds.

Not every small-world network is a positive or productive one. Economists point out that iteration can produce either a virtuous or a vicious circle depending on the perceived desirability of the outcome. In a vicious circle, the effect both accentuates and *aggravates* the cause, creating a downward spiral (Figure 6).

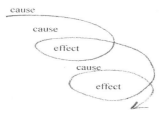

Figure 6. Vicious circle, downward spiral

A slowing economy causes a squeeze on credit and a fall in share prices, which produces a feedback loop that further slows the economy. In psychopathology, our little anxieties and irritations are magnified into big ones, as the very complexity of the system's associated memories, metaphors, beliefs, desires, sicknesses, flotsam and jetsam conspire to keep the negative network in place and make its bad effects worse.

And yet every component of an apparently unproductive system has value. Together, they constitute a vast treasure house of information far greater than many counselors, coaches, and clients suppose. How can a formulaic exercise like the Power of Six make the most of this underground store of unconscious intelligence?

As clients, one of the ways we know we have a problem is when we are confused. Too much information is jostling for our attention. A multitude of images, voices, values, shoulds and what-ifs combine to prevent us seeing the wood for the trees. The first steps of a standard Power of Six procedure (*A Clean Start*, Part Four) enable us to define a representative instant in that existential chaos, to confine it to a moment in time and to explore it at relative leisure, enabling the underlying pattern that holds it in place to be decoded and the solution contained in the confusion to emerge.

We have seen how any sphere of human activity is definable in terms of the number of clicks, moves, steps or questions that it takes to arrive at the particular bit of information that results in new knowledge or insight. My first experience of the therapeutic implications of this finding came in a research exercise in 1998, when I found myself responding to Grove's repeated question,

"And where could you come from?" by making a series of intuitive moves in spacetime that linked my then life in London to that of a 14th century yak herder in Outer Mongolia (don't laugh). I began the exercise at one end of Tompkins and Lawley's apartment in Highgate and ended up seven thousand kilometers away at the other end – in a yurt, as I recall, eating yoghurt. I had made, it so happens, six moves (Figure 7).

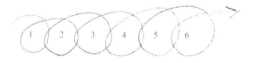

Figure 7. Virtuous circle, onward progression

I thought no more of this until a few years later when we were applying our findings in spatially based information to clients in therapy and Grove mooted six as the optimum number of spaces a client would require to network together before new knowledge would emerge. I was not convinced. I imagined that six would turn out to be an average representing a very broad range, and that the actual number of steps required for learning or change to emerge would vary enormously because of the endless variety of human difference and the endlessly varied ways we have of constructing and construing our problems. I was wrong.

Grove took the idea of sixness on a working visit to New Zealand in 2006. An American colleague, Rob McGavock, quotes him as saying:

> A doctor I knew threw me into a room with a patient and told me, "Here is someone I want you to work with, you have fifteen minutes." I then just started asking, "So what's the first thing?" "What's the second thing?" "What's the third thing?" and so on, up to six times. I was just amazed at how much the problem changed from one to six.

Later in 2006, he ran variations on the questions at seminars in the United States, France, and Britain. And in January 2007, the same New Zealand doctor who threw him into a room with a patient the year before made four of her consulting rooms available for Grove and I to develop the work as an integral part of her clinical practice.

In all this time and since, the number has proved to be remarkably consistent, with little variation on either side. I have now facilitated and witnessed hundreds of applications of the formula in seminars, clinics, trainings and my own practice, and I can safely predict that the majority of clients will need no more (or less) than six links to come up with the knowledge they need to resolve or ameliorate a wide variety of conditions. Most clients are separated from a state, sensibility, or life changing experience by six steps, six moves, six responses to the question, "And what [else] do you know?"

If there were a central intelligence at work in our lives, we would simply consult it and demand answers. These would be incontestable, because there would be no alternative authority and, who knows, perhaps no one would need coaching or counseling. But we are who we are, idiosyncratic and unique. There is no guide, guru, advocate or friend who knows all we need to know, though some claim to; no oracle or search engine that can come up with all the information we need; no therapist, however perceptive, who knows exactly what we need in order to allay or alleviate our particular problem.

And that is because emergent knowledge arises as the unpredictable effect of complex causes. It depends on what pioneering psychologist G.H. Lewes called, "a co-operation of unlike things." As the 19th century author of *The Physical Basis of Mind*, Lewes was an early contributor to scientific psychology. "The emergent is unlike its components," he wrote, "and cannot be reduced to their sum or their difference."

A single round of six questions may be enough to initiate the appearance of new insight. After a moment or two, or an hour, or a week of consolidation, the learning from the first round may be subject to a second round of six and the outcome of that applied to a third, a fourth, a fifth, a sixth, for the process, for the time being at least, to be complete; for the client to be able to say – though this may happen at any time before the sixth – "That's it," and mean it.

Emergence is never entirely 'complete', as we have seen. Its nature is to be ongoing. But there are completing conditions other than limitations of money and time that prevent an Emergent Self Knowledge session going on forever. I will have more to say about these in Part Three.

The Maori say that twelve and multiples thereof are the numbers of all the trails of the sea, the land, and the spirit, and that when all the doors of the mind are open to the houses of the heavens, the number is thirty-six. No journey of the mind is impossible; it is only a matter of navigation. The Polynesians who found their way round the farthest reaches of the southern oceans did not have sophisticated instruments. They knew only how to question the tides, the winds, the colors of the sea, the appearance of island-roosting birds like the frigate and the boobie, the height of distant cloud formations and the compass of the stars.

What emerged from their iteration was one of the greatest feats in human history, the discovery of thousands of new islands and the beginning of a new life for those who survived an uncertain and frequently hazardous journey. They went forth to discover the sacred line of life that linked the light of the rising sun to that of the setting sun and in so doing established a network of connections that gave them the wholeness of their world, its east and its west, its beginning and its end. And somehow, they knew that they did not have to *find* this knowledge. It would come to them.

§

In Part One, we reviewed the necessary conditions for the practice of the Power of Six and in the Paris salon we saw them in action: *Clean (Emergent) Questions, The Present Tense, Adjacent Spaces, Iteration, Formula* and *Sixness*. We considered how the formulaic procedures of the Power of Six work; how the roles of client and facilitator interact; how new knowledge emerges; and what is so special about six. In Part Two, we shall meet the numbers that are at the heart of every Power of Six process. Part Three defines the self-organizing network the numbers create. Part Four outlines a number of ways of orchestrating such a network. Part Five offers real-life examples. And Part Six looks to the future.

As client/explorers, you can trust the process: you know what you need to know and you will know when it appears. As facilitator/navigators, there are a few more things for you to take on board before you set sail.

Part Two

KNOWING THE NUMBERS

1 Proclaim

2 Explain

3 Reinforce

4 The Wobble

5 Crash and Burn

6 Out of the Ashes

Human beings betray you. Only the numbers can you trust.
Anon

Part Two Knowing the Numbers

Introduction

Number is more than quantity.   Gregory Bateson

The Power of Six is a living system and the numbers are its
heartbeat. These are more than mere numerals. Pythagoras of
Samos – philosopher, teacher, astronomer, and mathematician –
regarded numbers as a complete system of universal principles,
which represented the ultimate reality. Everything in the physical
world could be calculated and predicted through the meaning and
coherence of the patterns they made. The Romans developed the
theory. The natural or cardinal numbers 1, 2, 3, etc. (Latin *cardo* =
hinge) were fundamentals around which everything else pivoted.
Their importance was that they were not just for counting, but
measuring, and the measure was not merely the weight of gold or
the number of goats a person owned. Numbers signified *values.*

The more we learn about the universe, the more it is found to
obey numerical imperatives. "The diverse physical systems that
make up the cosmos," writes Paul Davies in *The Goldilocks
Enigma,* "are linked, deep down, by a network of coded
mathematical relationships." Numbers enable us to impose order
on, and give sense to, vast amounts of data, but they are also the
secret sub-text of any system.

Scientists say that for a proposition to be credible, it must start
from a principle, be supported by experiment, and be able to justify
and express itself mathematically. Six values drive the Power of
Six. They belong to a system that is both arithmetic
(computational) and algebraic (relational). The six have an
algorithmic (procedural) relationship with one another. They form
an orderly sequence, but they also work together as nodes of a
network, where the sum of their parts depends on the interaction of
the properties those parts represent (Figure 8).

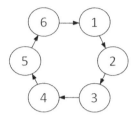

Figure 8. Six parts of a sequence relate as a network

Each component of the network has independent properties and a unique personality. As individuals they take something from each other and as members of a community they generate a collective intelligence.

CATHY is a graphic designer in her thirties. She is late for her appointment. Her coat is unbuttoned and her scarf trails behind her. Her hair is a bit of a mess. She puts down her bags and lets coat and scarf drop to the floor.

> I'm sorry, I couldn't get away.

I can assume that Cathy already knows at some level why she is here and what she wants. More importantly, I can assume that at some level her system knows how to get it. I need only ask her about that opening remark:

> *What do you know about that?*

She stops, sighs, hesitates, then answers:

> Well, I get panic attacks and anxiety.

Cathy has proclaimed the most relevant thing that she knows about herself here and now.   [#1 proclaim]

> *And what else do you know?*
> I know anxiety comes on and off and I don't know
> when and where.

She has elaborated on her statement a little.   [#2 explain]

And what else do you know?
I'm always frightened. In closed spaces, I need to know
how to get out.

She has found a wider frame of reference at the same time as
confirming and defending her original position. [#3 reinforce]

Already this is no ordinary exchange. The questions are focusing
Cathy's mind on the essentials of why she is here.

And what else do you know?
Anxiety is like fear, it's shocking, I'm sweating.

A flutter of dismay.   [#4 the wobble]

And what else do you know?
It always comes to me when I'm tired. I work too hard.

A loss of cohesion, a falling apart.   [#5 crash and burn]

And what else do you know?
(A pause) Well, I know about being quiet for myself, and in
a minute or two, it goes.

A reaffirmation; a reminder of resource.   [#6 out of the ashes]

From Cathy's last response, we can see that the problem is already
more manageable. "Let me introduce you to my six little friends,"
Grove would say at the start of his seminars. "Love them, they can
be yours too." Cathy's experience confirms that not all her friends
are nice to be around all the time.

The labels I have given them here – 'proclaim', 'explain',
'reinforce', 'the wobble,' 'crash and burn,' 'out of the ashes' – are
distinctions designed (or, rather, discovered) by Grove for use by
theoreticians and facilitators only. The client, it goes (almost)
without saying, has no need of these labels and need never hear of
them. Grove and I tried out other words and metaphors while we
were experimenting with the process, but finally plumped for these.
Sometimes I will use 'the barrier' to describe what clients may
come up against at #5 and 'phoenix rising' as a chirpier alternative
to 'out of the ashes.'

In a moment, I shall introduce our six friends in turn and you will get to know their different personalities and purposes. Meanwhile, we can see that they have taken Cathy, arithmetically and algebraically, procedurally and relationally, through an epistemological (knowledge related) exercise in *emergence*. At each stage, Cathy experienced a different kind of knowing:

> she began with localized knowledge at #1
> ("I get panic attacks and anxiety");
>
> she knew a little more about it at #2
> ("I know anxiety comes on and off");
>
> the scale of her knowing increased at #3
> ("I'm always frightened");
>
> there was a physiological shift to her knowing at #4
> ("It's shocking, I'm sweating");
>
> her old way of knowing was undermined and
> collapsed at #5
> ("I'm tired. I work too hard");
>
> followed by new, or newly realized, knowing
> emerging at #6
> ("I know about being quiet for myself").

A progressive pattern that is not confined to therapeutic process. It is a classic literary construction that draws us into a story and engages us emotionally. Jane Austen opens *Pride and Prejudice* with the confident, if contentious, assertion:

> It is a truth universally acknowledged that a single man in possession of a good fortune must be in want of a wife.
> [#1 proclaim]

The author expands on her opening statement:

> However little known the feelings of such a man may be on his first entering the neighbourhood, this truth is so well fixed in the minds of the surrounding families, that he is considered as the rightful property of some one or other of their daughters.
> [#2 explain]

Austen then opens up the frame to accommodate new information that confirms the existing position:

> "My dear Mr. Bennet," said his lady to him one day, "have you heard that Netherfield Park is let at last?" [#3 reinforce]

Just as things seem to be going nicely, a note of uncertainty is introduced:

> Mr. Bennet replied that he had not. "But it is," returned she; "for Mrs. Long has just been there, and she told me all about it." Mr. Bennet made no answer.   [#4 the wobble]

A little local difficulty. Mr. B goes back to his newspaper. Mrs. B feels slighted and her nerves get the better of her:

> "Do not you want to know who has taken it?" cried the wife impatiently.   [#5 crash and burn]

A potential crisis. What will happen now? Well, decency prevails: Mr. B accepts the inevitable and lowers his newspaper.

> "You want to tell me, and I have no objection to hearing it."
> This was invitation enough.   [#6 out of the ashes]

The narrative is back on track and domestic life continues on a note of renewal.

KEN is an executive in his forties, neatly dressed and anxious. He starts from a different place to Cathy and Mrs. B., but goes through a similar process. Here I guide the client through a *spatial* progression, which encourages him to embody his learning. Ken's dilemma is familiar enough:

> There is so much going on in my life.   [#1 proclaim]
> *Find another space.*

Mildly surprised by the invitation, Ken gets up reluctantly and shuffles around until he finds a different place.

> *What do you know from there?*
> Well, it all seems so important.   [#2 explain]

Find another space.

He troops around again, stops, then grimaces.

> *And what do you know from there?*
> Everything I see reminds me of something I have to do.
>> [#3 reinforce]

Ken's faithful friends One, Two, and Three have done their job of reassuring him that how he sees the world is, yes, how the world really is.

> *Find another space.*

An awkward friend, number Four, appears:

> *And what do you know from there?*

Ken equivocates:

> It's complicated. It's confusing.   [#4 the wobble]

It's difficult to tell whether Ken is irritated more by the question or his own uncertainty. It hardly matters. One reflects the other.

> *Find another space.*

Friend number Five is even less diplomatic:

> *And what do you know from there?*
> (Ken splutters) Pfff! Does it matter? (Shakes his head).
>> [#5 crash and burn]

Ken is at a point where many facilitators would stop and rethink their tactics in deference to the client's evident distress and his inability or reluctance to answer. Some would interpret Ken's "Pfff!" as 'resistance' and might even take it personally. However, here is a Sixth friend who is either unfeeling or has no fear, or is able to see beyond this temporary impasse.

> *Find another space ... and what do you know from there?*
> (Pause) There is space between things. I can make space.
>> [#6 out of the ashes]

Having had the opportunity to persist and work through his confusion, or irritation, or frustration or apathy, Ken has come up with a new tune to his old refrain and has learned something about himself in the process. He has constructed a network of nodes of information that encourage him to project himself beyond its immediate limits. His predicament begins to resolve (Figure 9).

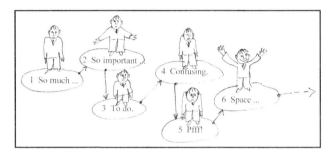

Figure 9. Ken's five moves, six knowings, one network

"The numbers care," proclaimed Grove. "Each one gives of themself," he explained, and then reinforced his theme: "and passes you on to the next." What do our six have to say for themselves?

§

Part Two **Knowing the Numbers**

 1 Proclaim

A word is dead
When it is said,
Some say.
I say it just
Begins to live
That day.   Emily Dickinson

What do you know about that?
Cathy I get panic attacks and anxiety.

What do you know from there?
Ken   There is so much going on in my life.

One pens a quick proclamation and nails it to the wall. One is a starting point only. It kicks off the count. As a first question, "What do you know about that?" (or "… from there?" or "… here and now?") is likely to evoke a fairly straightforward response.

The ancients didn't really consider One a number at all. It was thought to be a petty little digit, but acknowledged as essential if you wanted to get something going. The word comes from the Greek *oinos*, from which also comes 'unit'. In Pythagoras' system of influential principles, Unity was a Oneness that had no parts. It was acknowledged as the undisputed parent of numbers, a universal common denominator.

In fact, One is not petty at all, but remarkable. In the psychodrama of self-discovery, One has quite literally the principal role. This is no walk-on part. Without a first response to "What do you know?" clearly there could be no second, no third, and so on.

No sequence. No value-related progression. One is, by any count, wonderful. One proclaims. One pronounces. One states what it knows here and now.

To proclaim is to say that something is so without the need for explanation or evidence. One only knows what it knows in the moment, whether it be a statement of perception, feeling, or belief. One is not expected to be ahead of the game.

We can make an assumption here: that given the therapeutic or developmental context in which the question "What do you know?" is asked, the answer will relate at some level to a lack of something, or to something the client wants. The client is under no obligation to know exactly what that is or to be able to articulate it in so many words.

> Cathy I get panic attacks and anxiety.
> Ken   There is so much going on in my life.

Whether the unresolved need to which the proclamation relates is obvious or not, it contains the seeds of its own resolution. The Word at One begins to live that day.

TINA is a pale, drawn mother of four who turns out to have complicated issues around anger, but what she begins with is:

> I am very fussy about cleaning.

She smiles at me. However concerned she might be in her heart of hearts, for all the world it seems as if nothing is wrong. Generally, the voice of One has a matter-of-fact quality. Ms. Austen's opening line:

> A single man in possession of a good fortune must be in
> want of a wife

presents us with an ironic, unqualified assertion that cries out for explanation, contradiction, or resolution. What will happen next? Will the affluent bachelor do the decent thing? Will one become two?

§

Part Two Knowing the Numbers

 Explain

Can two walk together, except they be agreed?
Amos in the Old Testament

And what else do you know?

There is always more to say. One is impelled to step outside its own bounds. Austen follows up her opening proclamation with:

> However little known the feelings of such a man may be on his first entering the neighborhood, this truth is so well fixed ...

Two knows more than One, but not a lot. Two spells out and accounts for One, unfolds some of the folds of One, confirms and furthers the first steps of its precursor by making itself more plainly understood.

> *And what else do you know?*
> Cathy   I know anxiety comes on and off, and I don't know when and where.
> Ken   It all seems so important.
> Tina   I hate it when my children get messy in the kitchen.

In the Pythagorean system, Two adds Diversity to Unity. When there is only one thing, life can be monotonous – literally, one-toned. When a second comes along, things start to get interesting. Two is company, a pairing, a matching set. It takes two to tango. When Cathy says, "I know anxiety comes on and off," she is explaining what she proclaimed at One ("I get panic attacks and anxiety"). When Ken says, "It all seems so important," he is justifying his first proclamation ("There is so much going on in my life"). And when Tina says, "I hate it when my children get messy," she is attempting to explain her opening statement ("I am very fussy about cleaning").

At this point, the orthodox facilitator might be tempted to ask Cathy, Ken, or Tina to say more about how they feel, or when they first noticed the problem. This is the kind of intervention that practically compels the client to extend or embellish their story. Self-narrative can be a useful outlet for clients overwhelmed by events, but if left to escalate it will not change anything and may only serve to reaffirm the problem. The essential ingredients of a good story, after all, are content and emotion. Content is about what happens next and who says what to whom; emotion is about engaging the listener or reader. Thus, the narrator may dramatize or exaggerate the content of a story in order to engage the emotional expectations of the audience. If the client's storyline is strong or familiar enough, the facilitator will be tempted to follow it. If it is unusual or unfamiliar, the facilitator will be tempted to understand it.

Either way, the narrative itself becomes the focus of the work, a hook on which to hang the facilitator's own anecdotes, opinions, and judgments. This can complicate the plot considerably. Like rolling a snowball, the core accumulates layers and takes on density, complexity, and momentum. Eventually it may prove unstoppable and run out of control.

The model of questioning in the Power of Six, as in every Clean process, runs contrary to the conventional assumption that questions are designed to provide information for the questioner. The intention here is to provide information for the *client*.

And what else do you know?

Questions that are repetitive, non-interpretive, and consistently clean oblige clients to focus single-mindedly on themselves. The facilitator is a catalyst, not a participant, in this process. The problem does not take on unnecessary layers. It is held, suspended, so that the timing and tone of the facilitator's questioning will encourage the client to examine what they know about themselves very closely indeed.

The value of the second question, "And what else do you know?" is twofold, as you might expect. It confirms the self-examination frame of the process and at the same time points to the fact that whatever One may have proclaimed is not the only thing in town. Two is not up to any radical re-storying, however. Two is a natural conservative. It tends to come up with supportive and confirmatory, rather than contrary or complicatory, information. The job of Two is to explain and amplify One; to take the knowledge of One a step further.

Two is a necessary preliminary to adding a further (third) dimension.

§

Part Two **Knowing the Numbers**

 Reinforce

Space, time, and matter are a nice little threesome.
What's missing is energy. Anon

The word 'reinforce' derives from the Italian *rinforzare*, originally used in relation to strengthening a military force. The emphatic voice of Three confirms, sustains, and endorses Two, and adds a little something that fortifies, emphasizes, or expands the information. "My dear Mr. Bennet," declares Mrs. Bennet, "have you heard that Netherfield Park is let at last?" Three adds context. It takes a wider, broader, more global point of view.

> *And what else do you know?*
> Cathy I'm always frightened. In closed spaces, I need to
> know how to get out.
> Ken Everything here reminds me of something I have
> to do.
> Tina I criticize my children for being messy.

Cathy, Ken, and Tina are on the third leg of an iterative trip. The knowledge of the first response fed back to inform the second and now both are informing the third. Having endorsed Two's agreement to One's original contention, Three offers easy resolution. It believes it has completed the sequence by creating a neat little trilogy, trinity, trio, triune, triad, troika, or triptych (Figure 10). Three likes to rest on its laurels. It even believes its own press: "Three is a Magic Number" was a recent headline in The Guardian newspaper.

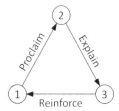

Figure 10. A neat little trilogy

If One represents Pythagorean Unity and Two Diversity, Three brings Harmony, the desire to marry those two fundamental principles. Three is a compound of both and found everywhere. The so-called 'Rule of Three' was put to work in the opening paragraph of this chapter. You might say it went into overtime.

> Three confirms, sustains, and endorses Two ...
> fortifies, emphasizes, or expands the information ...
> takes a wider, broader, more global point of view.

Facilitators who limit their questioning to series of three keep clients safe in their present reality. The special something of Three is its strength, stability, and inevitability (enough already). The triangle is reckoned to be the strongest and sturdiest of the geometrical shapes. Take away one of the legs of a milking stool and the others collapse. Three has a totemic value. The Iroquois of North America grew corn, beans, and squash together for the mutual support they gave. The corn grew high, providing a climbing frame for the beans, which provided nitrogen for the soil, while the squash contributed ground cover, which kept the soil moist.

It sometimes seems as if Three has authority over nature itself. Atoms consist of three constituents: protons, neutrons, and electrons. Matter comes in three basic states: liquid, solid, and gas. The earth has three divisions: crust, mantle, and core. There is a fated, completed quality to Three. The Sisters are Three, as are the Fates, Furies, and Graces ... Liberté, egalité, fraternité ... Veni, vidi, vici ... Turn on, tune in, drop out.

And yet, and yet ... the symmetry of Three can create mental inertia. *"La symétrie, c'est l'ennui,"* said Victor Hugo. It's not interesting. At best, it affirms the *status quo*; at worst, it limits the imagination. Three is not, after all, an irreducible Law of Nature. If we remind ourselves of what Cathy, Ken, and Tina have said, we can see that the reinforcements they have called up do not quite fit into the existing chain of command. In Cathy's

> In closed spaces, I need to know how to get out

there is both augmentation and a tinge of unease. In Ken's

> Everything here reminds me of something I have to do

and in Tina's

> I criticize my children

there is more for them to reflect on. "I *need* to know ..." realizes Cathy; "Something I *have* to do ..." ponders Ken; "I *criticize* my children ..." says Tina gloomily. These reinforcements are using another kind of ammunition. Is there a hint here, even in Three, that something is not quite right?

Left to their own devices, Proclaim, Explain, and Reinforce would probably call it a day at this point. They have gone as far as fair weather friends can. What will happen if we give up all pretense at polite conversation and *persist with the same question*?

§

Part Two Knowing the Numbers

The Wobble

Where you stumble, there your treasure lies. Joseph Campbell

Long-suffering Mr. Bennet declares that he has *not* heard that
Netherfield Park is let. His demeanor suggests that he might not
even care. If Three had reached the peak of a rising graph, at Four
the graph levels out and takes a dip.

> *And what else do you know?*
> Cathy Anxiety is like fear, it's shocking, I'm sweating.
> Ken   It's complicated. It's confusing.
> Tina I criticize my children for all sorts of things.
>   I criticize them too much

Four is a friend who lacks the agreeableness of Three. Fours are
unpredictable fellows. At first, they seem to confirm the
convergence of One to Three ... then they hesitate ... and when they
speak again their voices have an uneasy, even testy, quality.

A client's response to the fourth iteration can often be separated
into three distinct, if subtly rendered, parts. The first part might
begin by ostensibly supporting One to Three:

> Anxiety is like fear ...
> It's complicated ...
> I criticize my children for all sorts of things ...

There may then be a pause while the implications of continuing in
this vein are considered, whereupon doubt or discomfort is hinted
at or sometimes expressed outright:

> ... it's shocking, I'm sweating.
> ... it's confusing.
> ... I criticize them too much.

There is a distinct wobble to Four. Its knees feel shaky. Clients can feel suddenly vulnerable as the ground beneath them shifts. There might be a defensive reaction that manifests in irritation or indignation. There could be indecision, hesitation, equivocation, a wavering between conflicting feelings or courses of action, and an inclination to favor first one side and then the other:

> I dunno. I honestly dunno.
> Do I put up with this or not?
> I am struggling.

The mythical Beast with Four Eyes had two before and two behind, which gave it understandable difficulty knowing whether it was coming or going. The appearance of the Four Horsemen of the Old Testament heralded four great afflictions: pestilence, war, famine, and death. Towards the end of his life, Jesus referred to this apocalyptic vision when he prophesied a time of birth pains and great sorrows that would yet herald a new age. His disciple Matthew foresaw a time of considerable anxiety:

> The sun will be darkened,
> And the moon will not give its light,
> The stars will fall from the sky, and
> The heavenly bodies will be shaken.

Relative stability and resilience are replaced by unease. What is about to happen? It will not be a new age – yet.

§

Part Two Knowing the Numbers

Crash and Burn

Five to one, baby, one to five. No one here gets out alive.
Jim Morrison

Mr. Bennet's reluctance to speculate about the new neighbor at Netherfield drives his wife to distraction. "Do not you want to know who has taken it?" she cries. Oh no, we worry, what now?

At Four, the client crossed an emotional divide on the other side of which is the turmoil of Five. In Orwell's *1984*, Winston Smith is tortured until finally he grants that two plus two is not in fact four but "Five! Five! Five!" Five is fated to fall into disorder. The most destructive tornadoes rate five on the Enhanced Fujita scale. The Aztecs linked five to earthquake and fire. Five consumes.

> *And what else do you know?*
Cathy Fear always comes to me when I'm tired. I work too hard.
Ken (Splutters) Pfff! Does it matter? (Shakes his head)
Tina I get very angry with my children. (Tears come.)

Five may have the voice of simple difficulty (spanner in the works, fly in the ointment, obstacle to progress); or of deep desperation (end of the road, Armageddon, paradise lost). The client experiences a somatic shift as the awful truth is revealed.

In the fifth progression of the Power of Six, the resistance to acknowledging uncomfortable (unresolved) feelings that was felt at four is now more apparent, more present. The body may heat up. There may be fewer words.

The sturdy worldview of One to Three that was enfeebled at Four fragments at Five as the edifice the client has so carefully constructed topples under its own weight. Its defenses are dismantled. To dis-mantle is, literally, to 'de-cloak'. The protective covers are torn aside and the reality they concealed is revealed. Clients will say such things as:

> My head aches.
> It feels overwhelming.
> I can't change.
> It's gone all blurry.

'Crash and burn' is just one of the metaphors for what happens at Five. We may also talk about 'hurdles that have to be surmounted' or 'barriers to overcome'. My own preference is for the poetically redemptive quality of flame and fire, however, and the *emergent* nature of what will happen next.

If we deconstruct what Cathy, Ken, and Tina have said at Five, we can see that it is not quite the sum of what they were offering at One to Four. Cathy's

> I get panic attacks [#1]
>   +
> in closed spaces [#4]

do not quite add up to:

> I work too hard [#5].

What has hard work to do with panic attacks? For Cathy there is a relationship, but it manifests in a discontinuity rather than an equivalence. In the same way that Ken's

> Pfff! Does it matter? [#5]

does not follow inevitably from

> There is so much going on in my life [#1]
>   +
> It's complicated [#4],

though there is an obvious connection. While Tina's

> I get very angry [#5]

is not inescapably linked to

> I am very fussy about cleaning [#1]
> +
> I criticize my children [#4].

In each of these, the picture is incomplete, but the artist was unwilling to go further. The reasoning that led the client with relative ease from One to Three swapped sides at Four and is now the agent of its own destruction. Not as the result of any external assault or threat, but as a consequence of a relentless set of self-determining questions from within:

And what do you know?	[#1 proclaim]
And what else do you know?	[#2 explain]
And what else do you know?	[#3 reinforce]
And what else do you know?	[#4 the wobble]
And what else do you know?	[#5 crash and burn]

Just as Socrates would test and re-test his respondents' received ideas to the point of collapse before encouraging them to come up with a truth of their own, the walls of the fortress of #3 are undermined in #4 and give way at #5, leaving the interior exposed to the elements. We finally see what we have hidden from ourselves:

> Cathy Fear ... tired ... I work too hard.
> Ken   Does it matter?
> Tina   I get very angry.

What now?

§

Part Two **Knowing the Numbers**

 Out of the Ashes

But from himself the phoenix only springs:
self-born, begotten by the Parent Flame
in which he burn'd, Another and the Same. John Dryden

Happily, Six has the value of rebirth and renewal after death or disaster. In Egyptian myth, the phoenix was a bird of gorgeous plumage that lived for five or six hundred years in the Arabian desert until one day it rose as the sun at dawn over the waters of the Nile, built a nest of herbs and cinnamon twigs, sang a melodious dirge, set fire to the pile with the heat of its own body, and burned itself to death.

The poet Dryden saw heat as a transforming force. He was rather taken with the idea of self-renewal. From the ashes of self-immolation, a new sense of self – "Another and the Same" – emerges. The Aztecs considered the aftermath of the funeral pyre of Five as passing via death from one life to another. The Egyptian phoenix rises from the ashes with renewed vigor to live through another five or six hundred-year cycle. From the ashes of Mrs. Bennet's heartfelt cries arises a new understanding: "You want to tell me [about Northfield Park]," acknowledges a conciliatory Mr. Bennet, "and I have no objection to hearing it." Rapprochement. Renewal.

As clients, we may only experience the regenerative powers of Six by living and dying through One to Five, which is why facilitators must persist, after Five, with *the same question*:

And what else do you know?

Cathy   (After a pause) Well, I know about being quiet
       for myself.
Ken   There is space between things. I guess I can
      make space.
Tina   I should tell my children I love them, and
      praise them.

A new kind of knowing appears. Cathy, Ken, and Tina are living a script in which the appearance of the sixth character changes the whole dynamic of the play. The final *dénouement* may surprise us, but as in every good story, it turns out to be something we suspected all along:

I know about being quiet for myself.
I can make space.
I should tell my children I love them.

The fires of outrage –

I work too hard.
Pfff!
I get very angry!

– have long been regarded as the great purifier, not so much for their destructive capacities as for their power to dispel the demons of darkness. "Fire," declaims a Victorian encyclopedia, "is the heavenly mediator, which demounts in thunder and remounts in flames." Floods of tears have a similar cleansing function. The annual flooding of the Nile was once seen as a divine retribution for human sin, but its aftermath was to leave the lands of the Nile delta extraordinarily fertile.

In summary, we can say that as clients we use:

ONE to start things off, even if it doesn't always look as if we have started. We simply *proclaim* what we know.

TWO to *explain* what we know. We may add a little.

THREE to *reinforce* what we have said we know. We may begin to feel a mite defensive, having said all we believe there is to say on the matter.

FOUR to *wobble* as we are obliged to rethink our position. Doubt or contradiction enters the reckoning and the thing we have constructed begins to turn on its head.

FIVE to *crash* as we realize we cannot sustain our original position, and to *burn* as our world falls into disorder and the truth is revealed.

SIX to take stock and self-renew. The phoenix rises *out of the ashes*. New knowledge emerges.

Our surprising friend Six has a unique role to play in the sequence. Mathematically, six is the pivot of its divisors, which add *and* multiply exactly to the number itself:

$$1 + 2 + 3 = 6 = 1 \times 2 \times 3$$

The Greeks were inspired by this equivalence. They deemed six to be the perfect number in that it represented a kind of completeness. Bees construct six-sided cells for their optimal storage capacity. Every snowflake forms a unique self-organizing hexagonal pattern, an elaborate design with six (or very occasionally, twelve) facets. A cube has complete symmetry between its six faces. For Jung, a hexagram was a unifying symbol charged with powerful psychic energy that could reconcile opposites and synthesize contradictions (Figure 11).

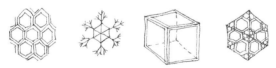

Figure 11. A kind of completeness

Six was the original number of colors in the spectrum. The discoverer of the constituents of light, Isaac Newton, had poor color vision, and is said to have arbitrarily added a seventh, indigo, for religious reasons.

Six repeats throughout creation. Trees and plants grow in a six-stage 'sequence of differentiation,' Dutch and French ecologists have found: six stages of branching (the sixth as qualitatively different from the first five as the sixth iteration in the Grovian sequence), followed by a seventh which is the first step of a new progression. In the next chapter, *After Six, or One Revisited*, you will find a parallel organizing principle at work in in the realm of human development.

Atoms of the element carbon, essential for all known living systems, have a nucleus of six protons and six neutrons, which together are made up of six kinds of even more fundamental particles, quarks. Six co-ordinates (Shift, Slide, Rise, Tilt, Roll, and Twist) precisely define the location and orientation of every base pair of a DNA molecule. And six is the number of co-ordinates needed to form a dynamic system of relationships around any given point (Figure 12). The number defines space itself.

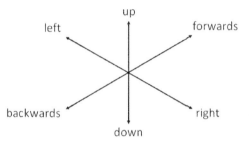

Figure 12. Six co-ordinates define any point in space

Six also happens to be the maximum number of times you can fold a piece of paper on itself (try it). I'm not sure of the significance of this, but it's quite interesting. And the chances are that you know someone who knows someone who knows someone who knows someone who knows someone else who knows a bus driver in Peru. A chain of only six acquaintances could bring you together, so be kind to everyone, because in the Pythagorean system, Six brings 'Justice'.

§

Part Two **Knowing the Numbers**

After Six, or One Revisited

Six days shalt thou labor, and do thy work.   Deuteronomy 5:13

One through Six is a necessary preliminary for what is to follow. After six iterations, the Power of Six has done its job and the mind is likely to be full of itself. Now another element enters the equation: a self-effacing seventh that allows the client a moment to recover, assimilate, and consolidate:

> *And* now *what do you know?*

6 + 1. The further question is more a reminder, a pre-arranged prompt from the wings. The client may have had a fascinating experience, but until something is learned, the experience will not continue in time. "It's like going to see a stand-up comedian," says James Lawley. "You can have a great time, but not remember a single joke the next day."

The tone of voice of the facilitator changes slightly to indicate the new mental space:

> *And* now *what do you know?*
>
> Cathy (After a pause) I need to give myself more time.
> Ken   When I make space, I get a better sense of what is important.
> Tina   I am not much of a mum, but a critical person. I don't want them growing up like me.
>
> [learnings]

"And now what do you know?" looks back whence it came. It encourages the client to connect with all that went before and to establish a base from which to go further. It is a 'learning', 'recursive', or what Grove liked to call a 'download' question.

("What do you know?" and "What else do you know?" were 'upload' questions.) Placing the word 'now' at the start ("And now what do you know?") pre-sets the context for the rest of the question. Some Power of Six facilitators place it at the end ("And what do you know now?") on the grounds that it concentrates the client's attention on the instant just before the response.

Either way, the question signals a shift from the *appearance* of information to the client's *awareness* of it by bringing the crucial mental resource of *attention* into play. We are prompted to notice something that is already calling us. Conscious attention confirms what we have learned and saves it to memory. Understanding and insight are more likely to be retained as a result.

Astrophysicist Martin Rees (*Just Six Numbers: The Deep Forces That Shape The Universe*) declares that "a tidy six" characterize the shape and form of the cosmos, but that "they still present an unsatisfied seven-ness of untidy loose ends and unsolved questions." In *Struggle of Life, or A Natural History of Stress and Adaptation*, Roelof Oldeman and his colleagues observe that after six steps of tree and plant growth, "there is a qualitative threshold after which another sequence of some six steps has to start."

Our clients' first positions:

> I get panic attacks
> There is so much going on in my life
> I am very fussy about cleaning

have advanced considerably by the sixth:

> I know about being quiet for myself
> I can make space
> I should tell my children I love them.

Now Cathy, Ken, and Tina need time to reflect. They have reached a qualitative threshold. There may be loose ends to tidy and interim problems to resolve. In the Pythagorean system, the number after six was a critical point, a climacteric. Pythagoras had a special sobriquet for it. He called it "the medical number." From here on, things could only get better.

'After Six', or 'One Revisited', represents a new spacetime when differences combine for common purpose. Seven are the Ages, the Heavens, the Vices, the Virtues, the Pillars of Wisdom and the worthy Sages of ancient Greece who met, it is said, at the Temple of Apollo at Delphi to agree on seven *koinai gnomai*, or 'body of common knowledge,' for inscribing there. The first and most enduring of these was carved into the portico for all who desired insight into their past, their present, and their future to see as they entered. It was the plain but profound principle that inspires this book: *gnothi seauton*, "know thyself".

The moment after six also has some of the qualities of zero, a Babylonian invention that signified a space between the preceding and following digits. The zero quality of "And now what do you know?" is as a position marker, a placeholder that serves both sides. It honors the preceding sequence and adds value to the sequence to come, just as zero on a thermometer is the point from which both negative and positive qualities are measured, and 'year zero' describes an event considered so significant that it begins a new reckoning.

There is a further way to confirm the new learning:

> *And what is* the difference *between what you*
> *knew at the start and what you know now?*

The reasonable assumption behind the question is that there *is* a difference. Facilitators who want to be hypercritically clean may prefer to ask, "*Is* there a difference …?" though I suggest this lacks credibility in that it patently ignores everything the client has been through in coming so far. But it is a choice.

The 'difference' question can be employed after the learning question, but more sparingly – not after every round, I reckon, but after a number of rounds or at the end of a session.

> *And what is the difference between what you*
> *knew at the start and what you know now?*

Cathy I know where the panic attacks come from and I can
do something about them.   [difference]

Ken   I'm more relaxed. I can only do one thing at a time, and if I want to do that well, I have to give it time – and there is a time and space for everything.

                                                [difference]

Tina At the start, I only knew I got angry with my kids for being messy. Now I know I have to show them I love them.   [difference]

These opportunities for 'downloading' –

> *And* now *what do you know?*

> *And what is the* difference *between what you knew at the start and what you know now?*

– are a time for the client to synthesize. A critical time to summarize and reflect on how far they have come before embarking on the next stage of the journey. What they know now is different from what they knew at the start and now they have a minute or two, an hour, a day, or a week or more, to decide if "That's it" or to go further.

§

In Part Two, we examined the roles of the numbers in the creation of an *internal information network* designed to generate new knowledge or change. Part Three will consider the component parts of the *physical and conceptual network* required for the functioning to its fullest potential of the internal network, and will examine how each part of the network relates to the whole.

Six days shalt thou labor and do thy work, and after six cometh a day of rest: a moment of consolidation and learning in anticipation of the task to come.

Part Three

KNOWING THE NETWORK

A The Client Space

B The Problem Space

C The Connecting Space

D Developmental Space

E Emergence

F The Facilitator Role

Network: anything reticulated or decussated, with interstices between the intersections.   Dr Johnson's Dictionary

Part Three Knowing the Network

Introduction

We know more than we can tell.   Michael Polanyi

A network is a system of interconnections. The interconnecting points in a network are sometimes called nodes, from the Latin *nodus,* meaning knot or 'knotty swelling'. I like this knotty swelling. It tells me there is something going on here that is potentially problematic, yet packed with useful information.

Every node in a knowledge network has discrete information and is autonomous. It self serves. It does not exist to fulfill some greater purpose. Yet when enough autonomous nodes interact, something different and interesting happens. They generate coherence. They become a unified, multi-functioning whole that is greater than the sum of its parts. Our six friends the numbers are individuals with a natural affinity and it is their neighborly interaction that prompts the emergence of patterns that none would be able to generate separately. Here they participate in the construction of a *physical and conceptual* network formed from the association and spatial arrangement of six distinct but linked components, A to F (Figure 13).

Figure 13. The Self Knowledge Network

Emergent Self Knowledge is not only numerically determined in a Power of Six process, it is also spatially and temporally dependent. Imagine the components of the network as nodes in four-dimensional spacetime. What you know depends on both where you are and when.

Figure 14 is a metaphor landscape for disentangling complexity. It represents the perceptual position of a subject/perceiver/explorer (the client in the space of A) in relation to that which is object/perceived/desired (represented here by a statement or drawing in the space of B); to the context so created in which both co-exist (the space of C); to the hypothetical further information spaces, developmental (at D) and emergent (at E); and to the facilitator role (F) on the fringe of the system.

A, B, and C are physical spaces established by the client through movement. D may be either physical or metaphorical space or spaces, depending on whether it is explored externally or internally. E is always a metaphorical 'space' – a further capacity, an expanse of the mind.

Grove came up with the principle of working with space from the limitations of working with language. He recognized, with Polanyi, that we know more than we can tell. Knowledge is tacit: wordless, noiseless, embodied, understood without being fully expressible. Its components may be densely compacted or widely dispersed within us. Sorting it spatially, therefore, can be the portal to other worlds.

Perceptions change with movement. By moving to another place mentally or physically, we remove ourselves from who we were and how we felt in the first place, as Noémie learned so well in Paris. When she found her place by the window, she was able to distance herself literally and metaphorically from the problem with her son over homework, and this allowed her to perceive the situation quite differently. The unresolved feeling was still there if she wanted it. All she had to do was return to the space near her son (her 'mother's space' as she came to recognize) that held it.

The notional boundaries that separate information in this way allow discrete worlds to co-exist. In particular, they protect delicate or tentative information from being overwhelmed by more overt or conspicuous information. The boundaries that define these adjacent spaces are not dividing lines. Trying to draw borders around mental images, memories, and metaphors would be like bottling air: there would always be more outside.

A clown may feel vulnerable behind the extravagant smile, but the boundary between vulnerability and extravagance has a porosity, a permeability, that allows it to serve both sides of the clown's persona at the same time. Information flows both ways across such a boundary. Clowns are both smart *and* stupid. The adjacency of the smart space and the stupid space allows states that appear to be completely opposed to one another to get along perfectly well. And if two opposing states happen to be located in spaces physically or conceptually far apart, a third space can always be found from which to mediate between them. The knowledge network is all-inclusive.

In a moment, we shall take a tour of the Self Knowledge Network in Figure 13, but first consider in general terms how its components do what they do. What is required for independent states to make a nation? For autonomous parts to make a whole? It is a process of generating increasingly useful information by combining elements of *repetition, iteration, and recursion.* Mathematicians and computer scientists use these terms a lot, but don't always agree on what they mean. In the context of Emergent Self Knowledge:

> REPETITION is a simple act of recitation, repeating something that has already been said or done – a question, a procedure, an unrealized need. For the client, problem patterns repeat and nothing much changes. As Winnie the Pooh said, "It rained and it rained and it rained." No change there, then, other than it would get wetter. (Figure 14).

Figure 14. Simple repetition: the only change is a diminishing return

ITERATION means generating something new by asking the same question repeatedly in multiple passes, where each pass influences the result of the last by incorporating feedback and learning. ("And what *else* do you know?") Iteration is **repetition + feedback**. The client takes into account the information that appears as a result of the first question in their response to the second, and so on. The output of each iteration becomes the input for the next and the effect is cumulative (Figure 15).

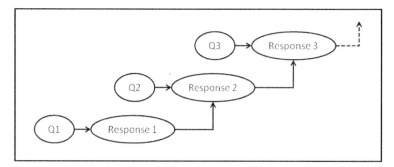

Figure 15. Iteration: a cumulative effect generates increasing returns

RECURSION is **iteration + repetition**. At the end of a round of the iterative questioning in Figure 15, the client returns to where they began in order to monitor how far they have come ("And *now* what do you know?"). The end becomes the starting point for repeating the entire procedure again. Knowingly or intuitively, the client will adjust their output each time, slightly changing what happens until the process is finished or completed.

Recursion does not imply lasting circularity with no conclusion. It is a dynamic process with forward momentum and an ending that depends on the needs of the moment. At the conclusion of Bach's Goldberg Variations for the harpsichord, the instrumentalist is invited to return to the beginning and play them again – *"zur Gemüths-Ergetzung,"* suggests Bach; "for the refreshment of the spirit." There will inevitably be variations and new insights with each 'repetition'.

In the Power of Six, it is the recursive, play-it-again nature of the questioning that creates an environment in which the client is enabled to work through a number of variations en route to an integrated solution. As the output of each iteration stabilizes, the client needs to do less, and recursion continues until, for the time being, at least, the client can do nothing more. A 'completing condition' prevents the work from going on forever. In the self-regulating world of the Power of Six, the completing condition will either be a limitation of time or a recognition by the client of "That's it, I'm done." For the moment repetition, iteration, and recursion have achieved their objective. The spirit is refreshed.

In the rest of Part Three, we consider some of the ideas behind each component of the Self Knowledge network. Part Four sets out in practical terms how the components may be elicited, facilitated, and encouraged to integrate. As Dr Johnson might or might not have said, the reticulations begin to decussate and the interstices to intersect. Space speaks.

§

Part Three Knowing the Network

A The Client Space

Figure 16. The client space of A

A is the four-dimensional node in which the client knows what they know here and now. The voice of A has a personality, an implicit or explicit desire, and a location that holds information about the client's preconceptions, prejudices, idiosyncrasies, beliefs, and values: here in this space, now at this time. The space of A is not a therapist-designated space, but one the client discovers for themself. In a basic exercise, the invitation from the facilitator is a simple one:

Find a space.

The client finds and inhabits the space of A in a primary world that filters everyday experience and from which their daily observations and decisions are made. The information contained in the space may appear in many forms, spontaneously or in response to:

What do you know from there?

Semantic (words) – "There's so much going on in my life"
Somatic (bodily feelings) – "My hand is shaking. I'm sweating"
Emotional (bodymind feelings) – "I'm anxious, fearful"
Behavioral (actions) – a cough, a gesture, the movement of a foot

Cognitive (thoughts) – "I seem to have a problem"
Figurative (metaphors) – "A huge weight on my shoulders"
Interrogative (questions) – "How can I get back to how I was?"
Indicative (physiological/psychological symptoms) – "My head/
stomach/heart aches"
Compulsive (habits, addictions, recurring patterns) – "I can't
stop myself ..."
Auditory (voices) – "Something is telling me ..."

And so on. Ideas, thoughts, and feelings that will be conflated with many others, and every one of them in a state of flux from moment to moment. To work with the primary world it needs to be stabilized, or the client may never get to know where they are in relation to what they want. The metaphor of space allows this jumble of thoughts and feelings effective separation and gives the client access to whichever they desire to find out more about.

SANDRA is a plump, upbeat secretary who has been trying to lose weight for years. Her first round of questioning has ended with a feeling of being "stuck". I invite Sandra now to:

Find a space that knows about that.

She stands up and inches round the chair, never going far, and eventually stops with her back to the window facing the door. The physical space of A that Sandra has found is a metaphor for the conceptual/imaginative mental space she inhabits in her present state of mind. If Sandra had all she desired or required, she would not be at A. To put it another way: she knows she has a problem as a direct consequence of being at A. She had to make a conscious or unconscious decision to place herself where she did, and there are obvious implications for this space being, or quickly becoming, psychoactive.

If this were a conventional consultation, Sandra would still be in the chair to which I had directed her when she first entered the room. If this were the only place in which she got to talk about the problem, it would inevitably become the problem space. Conventional questioning directed to the problem space tends to evoke a familiar story, a continuing description of the nature of the problem, which makes it less likely to be the place – it is almost certainly not the level – at which the problem will be resolved. Having been invited to find a space that *knows* about whatever is troubling her, Sandra can begin to disengage from it.

> *What do you know from there?*
> I have a struggle with yo-yo dieting. I start and stop, and can never really get going.

A temperature reading of the state of the system. Sandra is still entangled with the problem, but she has separated from it sufficiently to come up with new information. Her "I" is no longer "stuck". It has a "struggle" and it will "start and stop," but it is no longer immobile.

If I were to ask Sandra directly about the information she holds at A ("How does it feel to be stuck?" "Tell me more about the struggle"), it would only tend to confirm the attachment. If the client happened to have an inner child anxiety around stuckness or struggle, she would have to dissociate herself from the childish place in order to reply as an adult, a difficult thing to do from the position and perspective of a child. She might be able to see the top of a hill from the bottom, she might be able to see the bottom of a hill from the top, but she cannot be in both places at once.

My next question allows for Sandra's limited perspective, her limited mobility, and for what she has already said:

> *And what else do you know from there?*
> Something is holding me back.

Ah. New-old information. Sandra is beginning to explain the nature of what she proclaimed about starting and stopping and never being able to get going. The fact that she had located for herself the childish space of A gives her readier access to the child's information.

We will see how to take this move to A further in Part Four, *Creating the Network*. It can be very difficult indeed for a client in an emotionally distressed state to move mentally, but a physical move can achieve the same objective easily and quickly.

§

Part Three **Knowing the Network**

B The Problem Space

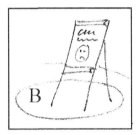

Figure 17. The problem space of B

A journey is often described as getting from A to B. Exactly how the client/explorer at A determines the exact location of their desired destination at B we will learn in Part Four. All we need know for now is that the spatial separation of client and problem is arrived at by inviting the client to give the problem a form through writing, drawing, or following some physical clue that has information about a space which is *not position A*.

If the client continues to talk about the problem, the original statement can easily be overtaken or obscured. Recording it when it first appears helps stabilize its form and location relative to the client. It is the start of establishing a relationship with it and making it more amenable to giving up what it knows.

Note that 'B' describes neither the statement nor the space, but the statement-in-the-space. The space of B that contains the statement will have information of its own about the problem.

The client may think of what comes up in response to "What would you like to work on?" as a problem, a mission, or a need, but I shall refer to the space in which it takes up residence as simply the problem space, in that it represents something that for the moment the client perceives to be problematic.

I have a fear of spiders.	[problem]
I want to rid the world of spiders.	[mission]
I want to lose my fear of spiders.	[goal/aim/objective]
I need the courage to overcome my fear of spiders.	
	[remedy/solution]
I want to be able calmly to put a spider out of the house.	
	[desired outcome]
Whenever I see a spider, my heart jumps a mile.	
	[statement (metaphor)]

The client's perception of the problem may be straightforward and overt ("I'm depressed"), or expressed in a well-defined outcome ("To go twenty-four hours without dusting the mantelpiece"), or disguised in a relatively neutral statement ("There's so much going on in my life" or "I am very fussy about cleaning"). In the Emergent Self Knowledge process, it does not matter what form the statement takes or what kind of statement it is.

Some therapy and coaching models work on the premise that every client, however intuitive, ill, or muddle-headed, should only proceed from a 'well-formed' (i.e. rational and positive) outcome. That would only be a problem if a well-formed outcome became an end in itself rather than a stage on the journey. Outcomes can only be formed from limited information about oneself and the world. In an emergent process, facilitator and client do not, *cannot*, control outcomes. All they can do is put in the time and the effort and encourage emergence to come up with what it will. The focus here is on *process*, not outcome.

A facilitator concentrating on seeking a client resource or a positive outcome may miss the information held in the negative things people say:

I don't want to live like this.
I can't do anything right.
I hate myself.

The space of B holds negatives perfectly well.

Whatever the form or type of statement, it will contain at some level what the client has and wants to be rid of, or does not have and desires. B offers useful boundary conditions for the information and provides a place to unravel its complexities. The problem is held in spacetime and may be accessed, scrutinized, explored, augmented, or deconstructed as desired.

It is worth repeating: B can hold anything the client wishes – an idea, an experience, a memory, an image. Even something like:

Figure 18. A problem at B

can hold at least as much meaning for the client as a carefully composed narrative. The fact of a *place* for B also frees the client from the constraints and rationale of linear narrative. Sandra ("Something is holding me back") can add more words, drawings, scribbles, and symbols related to past, present, or future as she likes, and she can add them at any time. B holds them all in concert. The information at B does not have to be coherent or sequential. It does not have to make obvious or immediate sense.

"The space of B is *listening for me*," Grove would say. "I hear what the client is saying, I see what they are writing or drawing, but I don't have to remember a thing". Nor does the client. The space holds the information on behalf of both.

Everything in Sandra's history associated with the weight problem that brought her to A has proved insufficient to resolve it. Her

    I feel stuck

is unlikely to be a pleasant feeling, but once it has been articulated, represented, and positioned, it is at least out there. Client and problem are in a differentiation phase. For what might be the first time in Sandra's life, her problem is seen and heard to have a *form*, a *voice*, and a *structural and spatial relationship* to her.

It is important for the client to establish exactly the right place and position for their statement. Some clients will place it close and face it head-on. Some will put it just out of reach. Some will turn away in an attempt to discount or ignore it. Some will put it at a distance, as if it were something they could never reach or resolve. It might be placed on a chair or the mantelpiece. It might be on the floor, a wall, or the ceiling. The occasional dissociated client will put it out of sight altogether.

The facilitator should ensure that the spatial and positional relationship of client to problem is well set and in *A Clean Start*, in Part Four, we will see how. It is a key experiential and symbolic act that sets up the psychoactivity of the rest of the session.

What happens when two things, any two things – in this case the client at A and the problem at B – find themselves in spatial relationship to one another?

§

Part Three **Knowing the Network**

C The Connecting Space

A third entity appears. A contextual, connecting, conflicting, or complicatory relationship space between A and B that we can, without too much deliberation, call 'C'.

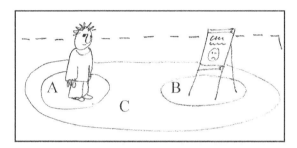

Figure 19. The space between of C

The fact that any one of us can choose or imagine where to place ourselves, actually or theoretically, in spatial correlation to anything else is the kind of metaphor that comes naturally to us. We have space-making minds. But all metaphors have properties that are properties of the metaphors themselves rather than solely of what the metaphors represent. The client is unlikely to see what *I* imagine here – a kind of oval space for C containing little circles around A and B – so I will not refer to them in those terms. Nor will I refer to them as A, B, and C. These are convenient stories for therapists and theorists alone. You may prefer to imagine A, B, and C as squares or triangles, as geographical features or military maneuvers.

All I might ask Sandra, in reference to where she has placed herself in relation to her statement, is:

What do you know about the space between?

C is the symbolic context in which the client at A perceives the problem at B. It is also the space that connects A with B, and the space that keeps them apart. C contains information about what has prevented the client at A from resolving the problem at B. How can we be sure of this? Suppose there were no C. A and B would be together and there would be no problem.

In trying to find a way to B, the client will come across something in C that inhibits them, prevents them, drags them back or creates a counter-force. C holds memories, metaphors, events, and experiences that need to be reconciled or resolved before a way can be found. It is as if our explorer were unable to reach their island objective, which is out of sight over the horizon, because they were at the mercy of contrary currents and winds. They set sail again, only to be blown or dragged back again (Figure 20).

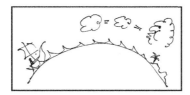

Figure 20. An unproductive pattern

SANDRA's objective of losing weight may seem theoretically attainable to her, but something is preventing her from actually attaining it. What she said in the space of A was:

> I start and stop, and can never really get going. Something
> is holding me back.

In the space of C, Sandra finds more information about how this pattern appears and repeats:

> I take one step forward and two steps back. The more I try
> to go forward, the greater seems to be the pull from behind.

The drag of Sandra's history is stronger than her present desire. She can imagine losing weight, she can picture herself looking thinner, but her heart and gut are not allowing it to happen. The implication she takes from her failure to achieve her objective is that she is just not good enough, lucky enough, or smart enough to make the journey, a perception that only adds to the problem.

I have suggested that the space of B holds more information than facilitator and client might suppose. The code to deciphering the problem at B will almost always be present in C. There are examples of how to tap both B and C as sources of information in Part Four. The facilitator may question not only the client at A, but also the client-created spaces of B and C in the certainty that they hold information too.

A, B, and C together constitute a limited, conflicted, self-replicating system. The parties are in what game theory might be called a 'Nash Equilibrium', after the celebrated mathematician John Nash of *A Beautiful Mind*. A Nash Equilibrium exists when no player has the incentive to modify their strategy *provided that* no other player modifies their strategy either. The client at A vows that they are doing the best they can in the circumstances and wishes fervently that the problem at B would resolve itself or that something in C would change of its own accord. Meanwhile B and C think it's up to A to pull its finger out first. The result, not surprisingly, is a standoff.

The parties to a standoff have three possible game plans: *doing nothing*, where they remain as they are and the conflict continues; *self-help*, where they do the best they can for themselves; or *mediation*, where they seek outside help.

Doing nothing is a common strategy, as most of us know. We may recognize that the system we have constructed is limited and unproductive, but it is at least familiar. This is both a perceptual problem and a problem of navigation. It is as if the Pacific islanders who wished to escape famine, over-population, or tribal wars at home had decided to stay home after all. Self-help, on the other hand, would be like putting to sea in a fog, when all you could see were your own outriggers and the water immediately surrounding you. The alternative was to hire a trained intermediary – their navigators had to serve long apprenticeships – to keep a watchful eye on the stars and the sun and the shape of the clouds. Information that lay beyond their immediate world. Beyond the space of A, beyond B, beyond C. The information required to complete the journey would be found elsewhere.

§

Part Three Knowing the Network

D Developmental Space

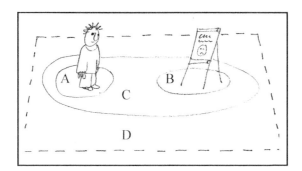

Figure 21. D holds information beyond the limits of the A B C system

Imagine the boundary that delineates C as the client-at-A's knowledge horizon. The client is unable to see beyond C because of the way the system is presently organized.

The client may be reluctant to accept that they inhabit a self-determined system. They may prefer to be looked after, 'held', advised, even told, what to do. The further knowledge the client requires in order to acknowledge ownership of their own process lies over the horizon in the conceptual/symbolic space of D, represented here by the dotted line around and including C.

When 'D' first came into the equation in 2003 or thereabouts, it stood for David, the therapist, asking the questions of a simple A B C system. David actually gave himself the lower case sobriquet of 'd' to symbolize the self-effacing role of the facilitator in relation to the rest of the system. Over the next couple of years as the model developed, 'd' took a step back from the facilitator role it had occupied and morphed into 'D', or what we may now call 'Developmental' space – potentiality space, recoverable information space not separate from A, B, and C, but surrounding them, suffused in them. D is to be found *within the client*, of course, as every such construct is, but outside the limits of the A B C metaphor the client has created.

D is a different kind of information space. In the world of Emergent Self Knowledge, it is more likely to be made up of a network of six, twelve, or thirty-six spaces. Information flows both ways, as we have seen, when the boundaries are permeable. D is the fourth dimension of the A B C universe. It contains information not readily available to the workaday quotidian world: some of it absorbed by the senses during every micro-moment of the day; some of it obscured in long term memory; and some of it fragmented as a result of traumatic events beyond present day reach.

If a client cannot get directly from A via C to B, D can provide any number of alternative routes. Indeed, D has information that can prove the entire A to B journey unnecessary. As a result of what is revealed in D, the objective at B may find its own way to A, or become peripheral, or found to be trivial, or disappear altogether. There is an example of this in Part Five under *Problem Solving*. The client, Silvie, could hardly believe that something that had been bothering her for so long was no longer an issue. After an intensive session of Power of Six questioning, her problem at B simply ceased to be.

Because the solution space of D lies outside the familiar limits of the problem domain, the information it contains may be difficult to locate. The client may have to *move* (better to sense the existence of D), or *turn* (and by doing so 'wind in' the knowledge of D), or *engage* with D in such a way that a different perspective on the problem appears. There is guidance on how to facilitate each of these in Part Four, *Creating the Network*.

In law, a deposition is out-of-court testimony. Every client at A charged with a problem at B has access to a D-position that will contribute towards resolving the case. The evidence in D will come to light, I suggest, because the client at A already possesses it. All client and court have to do is recognize it when it appears.

The Greek philosophers asked themselves how water could become steam or an acorn an oak unless water already possessed the qualities of steam and an acorn had all it needed to be an oak. The client at A has everything required to resolve the issue of B because *they already possess the information held in B, C, and D.* This is a key supposition of the Self Knowledge process. In systemic terms, B can also resolve the issues of A, C those of B, etc. Having generated the system, the client has personal ownership of it and under the right conditions it will work for them.

Plato believed that our subjective perception of learning was actually the recovery of what we had forgotten. Knowledge was innate. The question remained: how might we recognize and recover this elusive intelligence? Plato supposed that it could be recollected from the past lives of a person's immortal soul through proper enquiry; in other words, by asking the right questions. He writes about a wealthy young sophist, Meno, who comes to Athens with an entourage of slaves to ask Socrates whether wisdom is acquired by teaching or comes by nature. A typically lengthy elicitation by Socrates enables Meno to acknowledge that there are neither teachers nor scholars of wisdom, but that we must look to ourselves. By the end of the dialogue, Meno realizes he has always known this. It is not recorded if he passed the learning on to his slaves.

Placing Meno at A and his question ("Can wisdom be acquired by teaching, or does it come by nature?") at B, we can suppose that all manner of worldly distractions in C have combined to prevent this young man from resolving the issue. Eventually, Meno comes by 'new' information in D and realizes that it is not, after all, sourced from outside – in Socrates or any other philosopher – but in himself.

In a rather less discursive procedure, today's client is encouraged to explore the recollection space of D through a repetition of the question, "And what else do you know?" which can be said to project or propel their awareness into a series of bodymind spaces beyond, behind, within, or adjoining the more familiar spaces of A, B, and C. Ask the right questions and you will get the right answers.

It is as if the client were riding the questions as they pinged through the primary world into another dimension, in the same way that Einstein's thought experiment had an observer riding a beam of light to recover information that an observer watching the light go by from the ground could never access directly. From a new place or space, the problem looks, sounds, and feels different. It *is* different. When D gives up the information it holds, something changes.

§

108

Part Three Knowing the Network

E Emergence

Knowledge comes, and wisdom lingers.   Alfred, Lord Tennyson

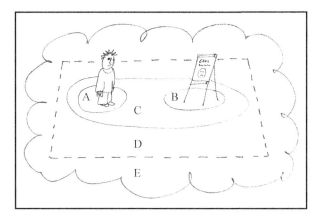

Figure 22. The emergent knowledge expanse of E

The conceptual expanse of 'E' permeates the whole system: the client at A, the problem at B, whatever has hindered or prevented the client from resolving the problem at C, and the recovered information space of D. This emergent world cannot be sought directly. It is not a state with a clearly defined frontier. The conditions have to be created for E to *manifest itself*, and this means a change to the limiting conditions set up by A, B, and C.

E represents the knowledge or insight that emerges at another metaphorical level, illustrated rather simplistically (Figure 22) by the cloudy line around D. Emergent Knowledge appears as a result of the systemic interaction of the other parts of the network. There are different theories about how this comes about, though none seem to me irreconcilable. Certainly, scientists and philosophers agree that emergence happens (see Peter Corning's *The Re-Emergence of Emergence'*). But how exactly? We are still not sure. Here are some of the prevailing views, though the language they use is so rich in metaphor that you must make your own interpretation.

Most theorists agree that there is no *central intelligence* in the network, no way of knowing exactly what is going to happen, but when the various nodes have *downloaded* sufficient information and it has reached a certain complexity, there is a *crossover*, followed by a *tipping point*, after which it takes on a new and different quality. Suddenly the network supplies an intelligence that seemed not to exist before. We gain wisdom by working through our apparent lack of it. We are wiser after the event.

Other theories talk of emergence evolving at successive *thresholds* of energy or complexity, just as particles evolved into atoms, atoms into stars, and stars into galaxies: new phenomena appear as the unpredictable result of an inevitable process. It may be the result of a *chemical-like reaction* in which existing bonds between atoms are broken and new bonds form. It has also been suggested that a network of nodes of information goes through a *phase transition* akin to ice crystals forming when water freezes: knowledge manifests in a new form comprised of existing constituents. Yet another way of representing what happens, and this was one of Grove's provisional views, is that the intelligence required exists in another dimension, and it is the relentless agency of the six questions that enables us ultimately to *punch through* conventional spacetime in order to retrieve it. Although Grove was firmly wedded to the everyday reality of his clients, he would occasionally flirt with metaphysical explanations. The information we require, he speculated, might be stored in a *parallel world*.

My own view is that emergent self knowledge derives rather more straightforwardly from both what we know that we know and what we do not know that we know. Throughout our lifetimes, we take in an enormous amount of outside information – researchers calculate more than eleven million bits every second – and almost all of it wordless, voiceless, fragmented, embedded, embodied, and lost to, concealed, or protected from conscious awareness. It takes up residence in an inner city teeming with old and new constructs: snippets, fragments, voices, images, feelings, and so on. The Power of Six assists us to retrieve what we need from this mass of scraps, especially, in a therapeutic context, to recover the bits that were damaged, fragmented, or scattered during fire, flood, and other traumatic events, and to reassemble them via iteration and emergence into a recognizable whole. The conscious combines with the unconscious and the knowledge generated effects a change in our internal world so that our reactions to the external world are different and our ability to function in it is enhanced.

In a 2009 paper, *Tracking Emergence*, Maurice Brasher suggests that our ability to recognize emergent knowledge is considerably improved in situations that are problematic when compared with ongoing non-problematic situations. "We are made more aware," he says, "and as a result, we are confronted with distinctions that were not accessible before." Then we are able to say that something new has emerged.

What in this context we call emergence is, I believe, a bringing into being – via an act of re-cognizance, re-creation, or recovery – of information present in a quiescent form that requires *a transformative catalyst* in order to thrive. A chrysalis holds all the information it needs to emerge from the pupal case as a butterfly and yet there needs to be a special event for that to happen. The catalyst in the caterpillar is a particular hormone, which is biosynthesized, secreted at a key moment, and transported to trigger special target cells. These recognize the signal, amplify it, and activate the process of transformation.

Our equivalent is the facilitator's questioning. It is the catalyst required by the mind to generate the synthesis, amplification, and emergence of learning.

§

Chapter Three Knowing the Network

F The Facilitator Role

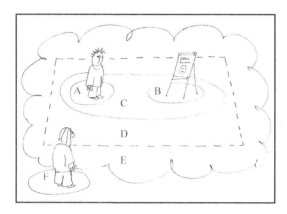

Figure 23. The facilitator serves the system
of which they are only a peripheral part

A catalyst accelerates change without participating *purposefully* in it. In a chemical reaction, the catalyst is not materially affected, but must be there for the reaction to occur. The catalyst platinum, for example, is a precious metal that actually costs very little to use because it works rapidly, so a little goes a long way and it is only necessary to have very small quantities present. A metaphor for the aspiring Power of Six facilitator.

'F' is in the service of A, B, C, and D, delivering the questions that generate the network and create the changed conditions for emergence, E, to occur (Figure 23). An 'opening', 'set up,' or 'upload', question:

> *What do you know?* or
> *What do you know about that?* or
> *What do you know here and now?*

An iterative question:

> *And what else do you know?* or
> *And what else do you know about that?*

asked five times in all. And a 'learning', 'recursive', or 'download' question:

> *And* now *what do you know?* or
> *And what do you know* now?

F takes on the burden of repetition that enables iteration to play its part freely, enabling the client to remain immersed in their own process. The facilitator's questioning has been likened to the rhythmic beating of a Buddhist drum. At first you notice it, then you don't notice it, and then it becomes a part of you. The Power of Six questions are percussive, value-free, and quickly predictable, so that clients are not tempted to get ahead of themselves by attempting to second-guess the next question, or to tie themselves in knots by dwelling on the meaning of the last. The questions are ultra-clean in that they can always be asked, they can almost always be answered, and they do not in themselves contaminate or complicate the issue.

Conventional questioning can draw the questioner into the content of a client's story in pursuit of a personal agenda: "I'm going to help you clear this up," "I'm interested in what you say about your mother" – remarks that chip away at the cornerstones of self-organization. The role of the Emergent Knowledge facilitator is to create a context in which the client is sole owner of what ensues. The facilitator has a discreetly protective function, poised on the network perimeter like an executive assistant screening visitors and providing the conditions for the CEO to get on with the work.

Here is an alternative metaphor. In 1871, Scottish scientist James Clark Maxwell considered how the intervention of an imaginary 'demon' working at molecular level might interrupt the gradual entropy of a closed system. Entropy is a measure of the disorder of a system that is not in equilibrium. The less energy there is available in the system for doing useful work, the greater the entropy. The facilitator could be said to play the role of Maxwell's demon by interrupting (and helping reverse) the entropy in the closed system constituted by the client and their problem.

The demon facilitator's primary tool is language. "All language triggers reactions," say Lawley and Tompkins in *Metaphors in Mind*, "therefore how therapists use language determines the way they conduct therapy." The precision of the language and the meticulous way it is employed in a Power of Six process, determine the internal direction of the client's search for a solution without imposing any construct or presupposition that might taint or tint the response.

As facilitators, we can be insatiably curious without adding to, reflecting on, discussing, or dissecting the information that appears as a result of our curiosity. We have no personal agenda for the client. That does not mean we cannot be partial. We may fervently wish there were less misery, frustration, and fear in the world while at the same time holding back on complicating or subverting a client's personal version of misery, frustration, and fear with our guesses and metaphors about how happiness or freedom might be achieved in their particular case.

This willful separation of desire and behavior can be a mental stretch for counselors and coaches who want to be part of the client's world. The more we wish to understand or to change what is going on for the client, the more likely we are to become emotionally involved. And there, as you know, dear reader, be dragons.

The discipline required of a Power of Six facilitator means abiding more than usual by the principle that we serve the client's system best by remaining 'outside' it – not outside the larger system of which client and facilitator are a part, for that is technically impossible, but on the fringe of the client's system, somewhere in the outer suburbs, beyond the last stop on the metro.

We operate from an assumption that a boundary of some kind exists between the client's world and our own. If we are lured or cajoled into crossing that frontier, it can be very difficult to get back and we may end up trying to fix the problem. Our clean questions alone have privileged access. They are like those little slivers of platinum that work rapidly and can be used over and over again.

There are a number of invitations we can make to set up a standard Power of Six session, but strict limits on the questions we can ask, as we have seen, and they must be asked without regard to the content of the answers. These creative constraints simplify the role of the Power of Six facilitator considerably, but they also test it and re-test it every second. Running the process at anything other than an elementary level is more than a matter of asking the questions and keeping the score.

As facilitators, we have to have our wits about us. Our phrasing, timing, and tonality have to orient the client to the location of their information and not to us. For that reason, we will have less eye contact with the client than in most other therapies. At the same time, we have to be responsive to every shift in the wind and the waves. We are like those wayfinders who learned to read the natural signs – the movement of stars across the night sky, the trade winds from the south, the steady swells of the ocean – without losing a moment's concentration. When the weather was unpredictable, timing was all. An abrupt change of tack and the vessel could capsize. Too slow and it would be blown off course.

The Emergent Knowledge facilitator has to develop a sense of the system as a whole. Fewer than six iterations and the journey may be incomplete; more than six and momentum may be lost. We need to be vigilant on behalf of every part of the system. The client spaces of B and C in particular find it hard to be creative or generative if left to themselves. We are equal opportunity employers of every kind of information.

Conventional facilitation can assist the client to move from where they are at A (present limited state) to where they think they want to be at B (desired state *as perceived from present limited state*), whereas an emergent process can change the fundamental nature of the objective at B so that a move there may be no longer relevant or necessary. When purpose disappears, there is true transformation. As psychotherapist Jennifer de Gandt describes it:

> We have navigated past all those fulcrums of development where we had to let go massive identifications in order to integrate our troubled experience into a new sense, the state

of being one with yourself and being one with the world. How well could David track through the tangle of myth and trauma and story and metaphor to the moment when we can look at the mind's creations and see things as they are – transient, faultless, inevitable, intrusive, instructive, imprisoning, freeing – illusions and revelations all!

Purpose vanishes at the deepest level of the work. The facilitator has a pivotal part to play in the transcendental moment. We may happily track the client's information, but not add to it. We may keep an eye out for those elusive glimpses of emergence, like specks of blue in the cloud, but not attempt to haul the clouds apart to reveal them. Instead, we maintain the organization and orientation of the search on the client's behalf. The facilitator is the artful agent of repetition using an iterative process to achieve a recursive end. This is therapist, coach, counselor, etc. as *agent* or *enabler,* assisting the client to get where they need to be – which will not always be the same as their original goal.

§

In Part Three, *Knowing the Network,* we took a virtual tour of the therapeutic arena that the Power of Six helps clients create: the client space of A, the problem space of B, the space between of C, the developmental space of D, the emergent expanse of E and the facilitator locale of F. What needs to happen for this vision to become a reality? What do facilitator and client actually do?

Part Four

CREATING THE NETWORK

Full wise is he that can himselven knowe.
Geoffrey Chaucer, 'The Monk's Tale'

Part Four Creating the Network

Introduction

The ninth century Persian mathematician Muhammed ibn Musa al-Gwarizmi, author of some of the most widely translated books of his time on arithmetic and algebra, gave his name to what a few hundred years later Chaucer and his contemporaries would call an algorism and we know as an algorithm, a set of rules to be followed in calculations or other problem solving operations. The procedures in this book are founded on the pioneering work of a native of the village of Gwarizm twelve hundred years ago.

The Power of Six algorithm includes a number of search patterns, or 'heuristics', from the Greek *heuriskein*, to find out. These are techniques for directing attention and enabling people to *discover something for themselves.* The facilitator-led heuristics to which I shall direct your attention here are the engines that drive the creation of a number of client-generated networks:

> A Clean Start – establishing an A B C system
> What The Client Knows – questioning the space of A
> What The Problem Knows – questioning the space of B
> What The Space Between Knows – questioning the space of C
> What The System Knows – questioning A B C as an entity
> Action Plan – following up on the learnings.

Six operations that make up the basic model. I shall introduce each in turn, suggest when and how best to apply them, and illustrate how they work in practice. They employ two key catalysts: *iterative questioning*, in which six-fold repetition supplies the driving force; and *adjacency*, the notion that different nodes or spaces to be found alongside one another hold different information. I shall use the word 'node' to refer to a hypothetical point in a mental network and 'space' to refer to a physical node formed by the client moving, though sometimes I shall use 'place' to mean both (Figure 24).

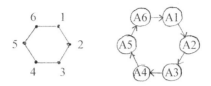

nodes in a mental network / spaces in a physical network

Figure 24. Networks of nodes and spaces

In a physical network, the spaces of A are unlikely to be arranged as neatly as this. A1 might be at the window, A2 near the door, A3 at the bottom of the garden, etc. I'm afraid I can't speak for the nodes of a mental network. Each node or space in the network exists independently of the others. The information it holds is there to be drawn on and developed as required.

A client may construct a complete information network from a single space by staying in one place, although physically moving to adjacent spaces may take less processing power and be more reliable. The concept of *adjacency* enables new information to appear readily and makes it easier to keep track of it. It can be difficult in normal circumstances for someone experiencing fear or anxiety – the first stages of a panic attack or a phobic reaction, say – to change state suddenly and feel fine, but simply by shifting place or position, they can separate from the anxiety and find a different perspective. The fact of moving from one space before stopping at another makes the next space *adjacent*, however far away physically it might be.

The facilitator guides the client through the process of shifting attention and position by introducing the simple iterations that allow the network to build naturally. Iteration is a means of drawing out information and building richness and complexity. It promotes an internal evolution of the network that leads to a collapse of complexity and the emergence of new knowledge or healing. A network of nodes or spaces is pretty much guaranteed to find a solution faster than any single node or space.

§

Part Four Creating the Network

Chapter 1
A Clean Start

Take the first step in faith even when you don't see the whole staircase. Martin Luther King

What is a 'clean' start compared to a conventional one? In a conventional start, the client talks about the problem, the counselor or coach responds similarly, and a relationship of some kind is established in which information is exchanged (if not always understood in the terms intended). A Clean Start is less concerned with the relationship between the participants and in an *exchange* of information than in maintaining the client's attention on themselves and on what *only they know*.

A Clean Start is a new start. It is the heuristic that determines the legitimacy of the rest, a prologue event that sets the scene for the main play, and its purpose is to establish the psychoactivity of the stage so that events thereon take on a life of their own. In Shakespeare's *King Henry the Fifth*, the Chorus anticipates the drama that is about to unfold between three key players: the English King, the 'French problem', and the stretch of water that links and divides them:

> Suppose within the girdle of these walls
> Are now confin'd two mighty monarchies,
> Whose high-upreared and abutting fronts
> The perilous narrow ocean parts asunder.

Two mighty monarchies – the client at A and the problem at B – with the perilous waters of C between them, all confined within the girdle of the consulting room. The purpose of a Clean Start is to establish a self-generated context for these three key elements as the basis of the questioning to come (Figure 25).

Figure 25. A prologue event

This three-part metaphor represents the substance of the client's internal construction of the problem. The client is recreating a critical moment in their rich inner world in an accessible form. Having discovered and established this construct, they are far less likely to complicate the issue by bringing in peripheral or irrelevant material. At the same time, the fact of having to move in order to establish the pattern that has been holding the problem in place is a hint to the client that it may not be as fixed in its ways as they may have feared.

There are two phases to a Clean Start: setting up B and establishing the A – B relationship.

A CLEAN START #1: SETTING UP B

1 *Choose the size of paper you want to work on.*

2 *Write or draw or find a way to represent what you want to work on.*

3 *Place that* [the statement] *where it needs to be.*

Setting up B in this way allows what would otherwise be an ever-changing internal world to be represented externally. There are no rules governing the way a client should represent their issue at B: they may write, draw, doodle, sculpt, mime, move, or work with a symbolic object. The paper-based example I use in this book is a familiar and convenient one that most people can manage.

Plasticine, play blocks, and other media can be made available, but most clients are sufficiently exercised with having to choose between different sizes of paper.

Equally, there are no rules governing a client's choice of pens, colors, where to place the statement or what kind of statement it should be. The process can utilize whatever information the client comes up with and in whatever form it appears. It can even be the kind of information normally considered irrelevant or unrepresentable – a cough, a sniff, the tapping of a foot.

If the client has difficulty articulating what they want to work on, we can always ask:

> *What do you want?* or
> *Why did you come here?*

Given the response, whether it is "I dunno", a remark about the weather, or a feeling that something is not quite right in their lives, we can simply say:

> *Put that down,* or
> *Represent that in some way on paper,* or
> *Put on the paper what the paper wants to have put on it.*

This last invitation can free the client from the self-conscious responsibility of having to come up with something meaningful. The problem itself is encouraged to express itself.

Facilitators may note for their own interest the *scale* of the statement. Is it scaled from the perspective of a child or an adult? Has it been placed above or below eye height? Is it written so large that the client might be feeling overwhelmed by the content? Or so small and tightly packed that they might find it difficult to unpick? At the end of a process of resolution or healing, we would expect the scale and placing of the end product to relate more to 'life size', a concept that will vary according to the nature of what is emerging, the personality of the client, and the physical space the client is using.

One of my clients separated out her information into three categories of 'coming into being,' 'adolescence', and 'adulthood', and placed all three papers around the room at varying heights to reflect what she called the "wrong sizing" of her life so far. She left little doubt where she was in relation to them at the end of her process:

> I feel my own size again. Not smaller than I want to be, and not bigger.

Another way of setting up B invites the client to maneuver with a blank piece of paper:

> *Choose the size of paper you would like.*
> *Find a space in which you would like to work.*

And when the client is in place:

> *Write down or draw something you would like to work on.*

There are several alternatives to these standard injunctions on the lines of:

> *Now write up your mission statement.*
> *Put on there something that represents the problem.*
> *Put on there whatever should go on there.*
> *And what words, marks, or pictures would like to go on that?*

All followed by the invitation to:

> *Place that* [the statement or drawing] *where it needs to be.*

My example is MARIE, a sales executive in her thirties.

MARIE: a Clean Start, setting up B

Marie sits hunched on the edge of her chair. Her make-up is carefully done, but I think she looks pale.

> I'm not feeling great. My work is getting me down, my partner walked out on me six weeks ago, I'm sleeping very poorly ...

I indicate papers and pens.

> *Put that down.*

Marie chooses a thick black felt-nib pen and writes:

Figure 26. Marie de-scribes

The physical act of writing enables Marie to describe (*de-scribe* = literally 'write down') the problem in physical, distilled, and tangible terms. This alone can be a way of loosening some of the knots of the problem and of separating the client from complete identification with it. Marie's "Down and depressed" is out there now. It has an existence of its own.

> *Place that where it needs to be.*

Marie checks, confirms that "Down and depressed" is okay where it is for the moment. The second phase of a Clean Start establishes the right spatial *relationship* between client and problem. Clients will typically make several adjustments to where they were in the first phase. There is a standard invitation to start this second phase:

> *Place yourself where you need to be in relation to that*
> [the statement].

The invitation is intentionally ambiguous. "Place yourself where you need to be" can mean either *where you are at present* in relation to the issue or *where you would prefer to be*. The client will interpret that as they wish. It is not the facilitator's job to decide which alternative is correct (either could be) or to differentiate between them.

When the client is in place, there are a number of standard questions with which to follow up. There is no absolute or obligatory order for asking these Clean Start questions. I have grouped them in a particular way in the box below, but it is not the only one possible.

A CLEAN START #2:
ESTABLISHING THE A – B RELATIONSHIP

Place yourself where you need to be in relation to that [the statement].

Are you in the right place?
Are you facing the right direction?
Are you at the right angle?
Are you at the right distance?
Are you at the right height?
Are you in the right posture?

Is that [the statement] *in the right place?*
Is it facing the right direction?
Is it at the right angle?
Is it at the right distance?
Is it at the right height?

Is the space between right?

One alternative is to ask the questions in pairs:

Are you in the right place?
Is that in the right place?

Some of the questions cover the same ground as others, but from a different perspective. There is a deliberate element of double and multiple checking involved.

If a client does not understand the invitation to place themself where they need to be, the facilitator can always add something on the lines of:

Will you be behind [the statement]*? To one side? In front?*

Which can be followed up by going into more detail still:

> *Is your body in the right position?*
> *Your legs? Hands? Should you be standing or sitting?*
> *Kneeling? Lying on the floor?*

MARIE: a Clean Start, establishing the A – B relationship

Marie has written "Down and depressed" on the flipchart and has confirmed that it is where it needs to be. I invite her now to:

> *Place yourself where you need to be in relation to that.*
> What do you mean?
> *In front, behind, to the side, in another room?*

Marie backs off and stands a few meters away looking glumly at what she has written. I ask:

> *Are you in the right space?*
> I guess so.
> *Is that* [indicate statement] *in the right space?*
> Yes.

I indicate with a nod rather than a gesture. Gestures can affect the client's perception of what is, after all, 'their space'. Marie might interpret a gesture as pointing to a place that has no meaning for her, or experience it as physically intruding into her space.

> *Are you at the right distance?*
> No. (She steps forward) That's better.

The client answers readily. In a live situation, the questions are not as strange as they can seem on the page. Marie is intent on defining her relationship to a present and genuine problem, an important task that takes all her attention.

> *Is that at the right height?*
> No. It should be a bit lower.

> [Flip chart is adjusted] Lower still.

> [Adjusted further]

Marie looks again at what she has written. The position of the statement relative to the client has changed, so I am obliged to run the second phase questions again:

> *Are you at the right distance?*
> Yes. (She moves a step or two further away) That's better.
>
> *Are you at the right angle?*
> (She skews herself slightly to the left.)

Any adjustment that changes the relative positions of A and B requires me to ask the questions again. The box on page 126 has a comprehensive list.

These Clean Start questions register in the client's bodybrain a split second before the mind is consciously aware of them, so it can be worthwhile keeping an eye out for small movements. When I asked Marie, "Are you at the right distance?" she answered, "Yes", but her body knew better: it was already moving to establish the right distance, which was actually a step or two further away. When she stopped and her conscious mind caught up, she was able to say, "That's better." Mind and brain had the same information.

Facilitators should not skimp on the time spent getting the A – B relationship right. The information that manifests in something like a little lean or a turn lasts a very short time and might seem insignificant, but just as a minor change can make a major difference to a person's life, a small move can mean a great deal. The step-by-step procedure of positioning A and B and the fine adjustments that may be necessary to achieve the right A – B relationship are themselves a part of the therapy. Self-reorganization is already happening.

However many setting-up questions a facilitator asks, there are only two basic conditions for a successful Clean Start: keep the questions clean and stay out of the way. The client's choices must be free of any hint of the facilitator's model of the world, so that whatever informs the client's writing or drawing, setting up and positioning, will arise solely from the client's model.

Marie continues to make increasingly fine adjustments to her position until she has established a definitive spatial relationship between herself and "Down and depressed" (Figure 27).

Figure 27. Marie re-calibrates

Marie in the space of A is now at the right height, distance, and angle to her problem at B, and there is a carefully calibrated space of C between them. This disposition symbolizes the client's mental construct as well as any physical analogue can. I may draw my own inferences about the choices she has made, but I will not express them. The form and content of Marie's statement, its scale and placing, the colors she uses, are items of information for her alone and will interact mindfully with every other item that appears during the session.

Another kind of Clean Start invites the client to move *before they have made any statement*. Information about the problem or aim emerges from its own journey of discovery (see the box below).

Clients conditioned to sit in the same place on their visits may find it difficult to move very far mentally. The place holds the problem and the problem will tend to configure itself in a similar, familiar way. The Clean or Emergent alternative – asking the client to choose where to be, whether the space available is a box room or the back of beyond – frees the bodymind to seek a different point of view, both literally and metaphorically.

MOVING FOR A CLEAN START

Find a space in the room.
Clean Start questions: *Are you in the right space?* etc.

What do you know from there?

---

*Is there another space you could go to /that would
like you to go to it?*

Are you in the right space? etc.

And what do you know from there?

Repeat these three questions five times in all, then:

And now *what do you know?*

Choose the size of paper you want to work on ... etc.
[Continue with the standard Clean Start invitation]

My example is STEVE, who is in his late twenties; a highly-strung young man who is finding it difficult to keep still.

STEVE: moving for a Clean Start

Steve enters one of the consulting rooms at the medical practice where Grove and I are running an outpatient clinic. Sometimes we work in tandem with patients and sometimes separately. Sometimes I observe and sometimes I take over while David has a break or goes to check on another patient. We have use of four consulting rooms, a luxury that enables us to work with up to four people at the same time when the clinic is busy. One patient might be drawing up a statement or considering how to place several statements in relation to each other; another might be pondering between rounds on what they have learned or compiling an action plan: all things that can be done (and often are better done) unaccompanied.

Co-facilitation, alternate facilitation, and multiple facilitation can work perfectly well in a process where the client is dependent less on their relationship with the therapist than with their own information.

> *Co-facilitation*: both facilitators are present. Either may question the client, though it's best not to switch around frequently. If the client has agreed to the arrangement, and if the facilitators are experienced and in rapport, the client's attention will be undivided.

> *Alternate facilitation*: one facilitator takes over from the other and works separately with the client. Very little information is required to take over a Power of Six session: the number of the last question or of the last round is usually enough. I do not recommend alternating repeatedly.

> *Multiple facilitation*: one facilitator works with two or more clients in separate spaces. Clients should be left only when there is a project for them to accomplish between rounds. Time to oneself can be beneficial during an extended session. It allows the client to process at their own pace and is a reminder of self responsibility.

Steve says he has no idea why the practice doctor has referred him for psychotherapy, but now he is here, he reckons, he has nothing to lose. He is unconcerned about having two therapists present and responds immediately to David's invitation to "Find a space in the room." Steve strides around and eventually stops. David asks:

> *Is that the right space?*

Steve falters slightly.

> I guess not quite. (He adjusts the direction he is facing)

> *Is that the right space?*
> Yeh.

> *Are you facing in the right direction?*

Steve tries out different directions before settling on one.

> *Is that the right direction?*
> Near enough. (He adjusts) Not really.

There is something about Steve's restlessness and ambivalence that prompts David to suggest he keeps moving:

> *Keep moving until you know you are in the right place*
> *and position.*

Steve moves, sits, adjusts his long legs, stands, moves again and finally confirms that he is good where he was in the first place. David runs through the standard Clean Start questions ("Are you in the right place / position/ at the right height/angle?" etc.), prompting Steve to make several more adjustments, then:

> *And what do you know from there?*
> I can recognize my discomfort.   [#1 proclaim]

I had supposed that Steve was going along with us today because he was curious and had nothing better to do. Now I am reminded how quickly a single Clean question can take hold. The fact that David has taken Steve's restlessness for granted and has neither challenged nor attempted to interpret it has prompted this 're-cognization' by Steve of its associated problems.

> *Is there another space you can go to?*
> (Steve moves readily, tries to settle)
>
> *And what do you know from there?*
> It's emotional, it's beyond the rights and wrongs
> of my problem.   [#2 explain]

He ponders this. It seems to be new information. Perhaps for the first time in his life the client is considering the connection between his inner and outer selves. Now Steve moves without asking and answers the next question for himself:

> Why is this? I can't help myself, I'm never still, and it's
> not doing me any good. Why am I like this? *[#3 reinforce]*

David may be tempted to speculate or to join in the 'story', but says only:

Is there another space you can move to?

After three further moves and responses to the follow-up question, "And what do you know from there?" Steve finds a link that leads to a learning. He tells us about a series of compulsive habits, none of which he believed were related before. The latest involves checking the soles of his shoes for chewing gum every few minutes, something he says he would rather not do. When it comes to the re-validation question "And now what do you know?" he is finally able to say:

Yeh, I can let go. [learning]

Which does not indicate completion, I note, but knowledge of possibility, as good a starting point as any for a second round.

The act of processing the fine distinctions intrinsic to the Clean Start questions and having to make multiple, finely judged decisions in order to respond, is likely to be a microcosm of how a client lives their life. The number of adjustments Steve has found himself making before establishing a definitive A B C pattern may be a reflection of the extent to which he has been wrestling with the inner problem ("my discomfort, it's emotional") outside.

MARIE's Clean Start in relation to "Down and depressed" has given her problem a form and a location, and now she has something on which to focus. Every one of the issues associated with her statement is likely to have been represented in the two simple but mindful acts of writing what she did and positioning herself in relation to what she wrote. At the start, client and problem were inextricably linked. In positioning and repositioning herself, Marie has begun to differentiate herself from the problem. Now she is on the threshold of discovering something new. As her facilitator, I have several choices (Figure 28):

I can ask Marie at A what she knows about "Down and Depressed" at B
(see Chapter 2 of Part Four, *What the Client Knows*);

I can ask "Down and Depressed" at B to say what it
knows about itself
(Chapter 3, *What the Problem Knows*);

I can ask the space of C that lies between and around
Marie at A and her statement at B a similar question
(Chapter 4, *What the Connecting Space Knows*);

I can even interrogate A B C as a whole
(Chapter 5, *What the System Knows*).

Figure 28. Facilitator choices: question A, B, or C, or A B C as a whole

These are only the obvious possibilities. Systemically, I have
many more choices. I can ask what B knows about A ("What does
that know about you?"); I can ask what C knows about B ("What
does that space know about that?"); and so on. Nineteen possible
strategies and for each at least three theoretical alternatives:
stationary, moving, and turning. (There is more about turning in
the next chapter.) Fifty-seven varieties and counting.

What criteria should I use in deciding what line to take with
Marie? One thing that helps is my sense of the location of what
Grove used to characterize as "Whose voice [A's, B's, or C's] is
shouting the loudest?" This early criterion changed to considering
the location of *the highest density of information*, which allows for
the fact that the least heard may have the most unsaid. One of the

functions of a facilitator is to locate these quiet voices or 'weak links' and give them an opportunity to speak for themselves.

There are several other strategies I can employ. If the client seems to be cognitively or verbally oriented, I might begin linguistically and question A on the spot. If the 'density' of the information seems to be in the client's body – if they seem to be more emotionally or kinesthetically disposed – I might invite A to move. If the weight or substance seems to be in the statement itself, I might invite the client to move B or to ask B what it knows about itself. And if the client's information seems to be far-off, or if they are spiritually or otherworldly inclined, I might introduce the spiral/turning model of questioning (see Chapter 2 coming up), which in effect asks the client to notice the direction of the *source* of their information. Finally, I can invite the client to choose for themselves by asking something on the lines of the Clean Language question: "And where is your attention drawn?" or "And where is your attention now?"

My clues in this case are in the way Marie has responded so far. What has come more naturally to her: talking or moving, writing or drawing? Has she kept her problem at arm's length or close by? I have a sense that Marie is emotionally articulate and yet not very mobile. Should I invite her then to leave her zone of familiarity at A to explore the shifting sands of B or the turbulent waters of C? Or might it be too soon for that?

There are no definitive answers to questions like this! I am left with my intuition, or what some call 'trusting your feelings in familiar situations.' How familiar do you need to be? Recent neurological research on intuition indicate that the brain regions responsible for *making* decisions are the same regions that receive the sensory signals necessary for *considering* the decisions. There is no separation of function. To put it another way: if I let my frontal lobes in on the act, they will probably complicate the issues unnecessarily. The best way of making these decisions is not to think about them too much. For the moment, I shall question Marie where she is.

§

Part Four Creating the Network

Chapter 2
What The Client Knows: Stationary at A
Moving from A
Turning at A

Who knows others is learned. Who knows themself is wise.
Lao Tse

After deciding to question the client directly at A, I have a further choice to make. I can employ any one of three standard search and discovery patterns (Figure 29).

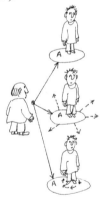

Figure 29. Facilitator choices when questioning
the client at A: stationary, moving, or turning

Stationary at A

Questioning the client directly in the space of A is generally indicated when they are able to express themself readily, or are unable to move easily, or have rather more to say than they can conveniently put on paper.

> QUESTIONING THE CLIENT AT A
>
> *What do you know here and now / from there?*
>
> *And what else do you know?*
> [Repeat this question 5 times in all]
>
> *And* now *what do you know?*

MARIE is my example again, although she is typical only in the sense that every client is unique. In each case study in this practical chapter, I suggest you attend more to the form of the procedure and the nature of the numbers than to the content of the response. If you are very smart you might be able to do all three at the same time, but I wouldn't count on it.

Marie is standing in her final Clean Start position, a meter or two away from the flipchart. I refer to her statement and ask:

> *What do you know here and now?*
> What it says. I feel down and depressed.   [#1 proclaim]

Adding "here and now" is a variation on the standard opener and emphasizes the present moment, the only medium in which change can happen. Maintaining the client's attention on the present is more difficult than one might suppose. A study in 2008 by Harvard psychologist Randy Buckner concluded that unless our brains are called upon to do something specific, their default state is 'time travel': we wander off into the past or lose ourselves in the future, a finding that underlines the importance of timing and phrasing the questions in order to maintain the client's attention on what is happening for them *now* at this time, *here* in this place.

> *And what else do you know?*
> I feel kind of empty. The outlook is bleak.   [#2 explain]

> *And what else do you know?*
> It feels like not just in the short term, but in the long
> term too.   [#3 reinforce]

Marie's "outlook", short term or long term, is a future projection.

> *And what else do you know?*
> Perhaps I have to resign myself to it.   [#4 the wobble]
>
> *And what else do you know?*
> (Shakes her head) I can't see it getting better.
> It's a state I can't change.   [#5 crash and burn]

Still in the hereafter, a time that supposes the future is contingent upon the present. It is so, Marie believes, therefore it will be so.

> *And what else do you know?*

Marie pauses. When she speaks again, her voice has a lighter tone.

> Well, I don't want to over-exaggerate the minuses.
>   [#6 out of the ashes]

Instead of projecting herself further into a gloomy future, Marie is using the relentless here and now-ness of the questioning to direct her attention to her present state. When the new information ("I don't want to over-exaggerate the minuses") has had a moment to sink in, I speak a little more slowly, with a change of emphasis. My final question remains in – in fact, emphasizes – the present:

> *And* now *what do you know?*
> Well, accepting it can make it better.   [learning]
> (I nod towards the flipchart) *Put that down.*

Under "Down and Depressed," Marie writes, "Accepting it can make it better."

Clients can be invited to record their responses at any time. It helps some people to have a continuous record of their process. And using auditory, kinesthetic, and visual modes of expression in combination as they hear what they say, feel what they write, and see the result, is likely to prompt more bodymind connections and leave a stronger memory trace. (Eva's multi-modal process in Part Five, *Relationship*, is another example.

Clients who have a great deal to say for themselves, on the other hand, or who are reluctant to write, or feel held back by taking the time to write, can be invited to update their statements at longer intervals: at the end of a round, say, or at the end of the session.

Moving from A

As an alternative to facilitating Marie to create an internal network of information in the space of A, I can invite her to set up a physical network by moving to adjacent spaces in the domain of D. I have to allow that she may be reluctant to move, or may find it difficult to move, and yet moving might be the breakthrough she didn't know she needed.

Move to another space.

Inviting a client to find a new space would be indicated if they had shown an instinctive preference for moving rather than staying put, or if there was a distinct paucity of information emerging from the stationary place. The only rule I suggest you abide by here, and it applies to any Power of Six process, is not to change heuristics mid-stream. The iterative power of the sequence will be compromised by mixing moving and stationary questions in the same round. I strongly recommend completing a set of six using the same heuristic before introducing another.

An invitation to move should not come across as an instruction. Marie has to decide for herself whether she wishes to move or not. An alternative to "Move to another space" would be:

Is there another space you can go to?

MOVING THE CLIENT FROM A

Is there another space you can go to?
[Or] *Move to another space.*

And what do you know from there?

[Repeat invitation and question 5 more times]

And now *what do you know?*

I offer no advice about the choice between "Is there …?" or "Move to …" Your tone of voice will make either into an invitation. I would only say that having started a round with one version, you should continue with it to the end.

MARIE is ready for a second round to follow up her learning ("Accepting it can make it better") from the first.

> *Is there another space you can go to?*

Marie moves away from the flipchart and changes her angle to it slightly.

> *And what do you know from there?*
> It looks different.   [#1 proclaim]
>
> *And is there another space you can go to?*
> (She moves another step away)
>
> *And what do you know from there?*
> I was too close.   [#2 explain]
>
> *And is there another space you can go to?*
> (She moves further away still)
>
> *And what do you know from there?*
> The writing is smaller.   [#3 reinforce]
>
> *And is there another space you can go to?*
> (She moves half a step further)
>
> *And what do you know from there?*
> The only thing is the ... because it's smaller,
> maybe I'm ignoring it.   [#4 the wobble]

In Marie's first round, her fourth response included the word "perhaps". Here the word "maybe" has appeared. Expressions like this are sure indicators of a loosening in the fixed nature of a client's perceptions. Others are hesitations, negative conjunctions, doubt, and unease, however expressed.

> *And is there another space you can go to?*
> (Marie moves a significant step away)

And what do you know from there?
Nothing. It's gone all blurry.   [#5 crash and burn]

And is there another space you can go to?
(A further step back)

And what do you know from there?
From a distance it seems less threatening.
                                               [#6 out of the ashes]

And now *what do you know?*
It's all a lot calmer from far away.   [learning]
Put that down.

Figure 30. Marie after two rounds

I am not suggesting that Marie's "Down and Depressed" has lifted after two rounds of questioning, but she has found a place of calm for herself without a single suggestion from me and without one empathic reflection. My final invitation to "put that down" gives her the opportunity to reflect on herself. This "calmer now" place will serve as a base for the next stage of her journey.

Turning at A

When Grove was developing the methodology of Clean Space, he made a remarkable discovery: that a problem state could ameliorate or disappear altogether if the client were invited to face in another direction.

Here is another way of working with the client in the space of A: invite them to turn a few degrees of a circle at a time, in a clockwise or anti-clockwise direction as they choose, and to stop whenever new information appears.

Some points on the circle will hold information and some won't. The facilitator has a hand on the steering at the start of the exercise, but the touch is light and in some cases can be removed altogether. Clients often learn to turn to a measure of their own. When that happens, all a facilitator has to do is stay out of the way and keep count.

CLIENT TURNING AT A

Turn slowly in either direction until you know something else.

And what do you know there?

_____

Keep turning until you know something else.

And what do you know there?

[Repeat invitation and question 4 more times]

And now *what do you know?*

Turning is an unusual way of working, even by Power of Six standards, and is more likely to be more effective if the client has already been through stationary and moving rounds and is familiar with the process. Then it just becomes another way.

LORRAINE is a 44-year old restaurant server who suffers from abdominal discomfort, back pain, and anxiety. She continues to stand rather than sit while I take her through a round of stationary questioning. At the end, she has learned that:

> There's more to this than meets the eye here. Does this
> go back to my Dad and his pain?   [learning #1]

Anyone trained in the promise of ambiguity will understand that the only possible Clean question one would want to ask at this point – and David chips in to ask it – is:

And what kind of back does this go back to?

Lorraine responds immediately:

> Well, my Dad's. He was always telling us to sit up straight.
> Now he's flat on his back in intensive care.

The end of a round is an opportunity to ask clarifying questions. If the questions are Clean, they will not prejudice the next set of Six. I have experimented with introducing Clean Language questions into the middle of an iterative six, but it muddied the waters considerably and I would not recommend it.

At the end of a second stationary round, Lorraine comes up with another learning:

> I realize that Dad's end is near and that will mean big
> changes for me.   [learning #2]

She goes on to talk about her mother for the first time and puzzles why she treated Lorraine in the way that she did:

> My whole life she never said she loved me or even liked me.
> What did I do wrong?

There is something about Lorraine's position, standing stock-still and gazing into the distance, which prompts David to invite her now to:

> *Turn slowly in either direction until you know something*
> *else.* (Lorraine makes a quarter-turn clockwise and stops)
>
> *What do you know from there?*
> Ah, what I always knew but haven't said.
>
> *Keep turning until you know something else.*
> (She makes another quarter-turn)
>
> *And what do you know from there?*
> I feel like a fool for not saying.

Lorraine does not wait for another invitation. She turns of her own volition, nods and stops whenever new information appears. One turn merges into the next and both David and I lose count. It can happen. Lorraine has discarded her L-plates and is motoring pretty much on her own now.

> I've never exposed how I feel like this before. I'd like to know the answers to some questions ...   [turns]
>
> My life's been a ... apart from my husband and children ... you have your ups and downs ...   [turns]
>
> I'm not looking forward to the day my Dad dies ... so many uncles and aunts passing away ... my husband's heart attack, a big scare ...   [turns]
>
> Hey world, stop, I want to get off ... I dunno ... I honestly dunno ... I feel like I'm locked in a room and I wanna get out ...   [turns]
>
> I just kind of feel tired ... I'd like to go to Egypt ...   [turns]
>
> I don't wanna see my Dad suffer any more ... he's been very sick over the years ... my Mum was a real bitch and when she died it was really peacefully, quickly, and he's been dragged through all these illnesses – deep vein thrombosis, leukemia, heart attack ...   [turns]
>
> I know there's nothing I can do about it.   [stops]

Lorraine has taken herself through a round or two on her own and has ended up facing the same direction in which she began. She seems to have reached a place of reflection now, so I ask:

> *And* now *what do you know?*
> I have to collect the money from my brothers and cousins to pay for the funeral.   [learning #3]

A literal and metaphorical turning point. Lorraine tells me that the cost of the funeral has been a major issue that she has been doing her best to avoid. A unique feature of the turning exercise is that the client is obliged to face in a number of different directions. It would be unusual if at least one of these were not one they had been avoiding.

Lorraine goes on to make an action plan (Chapter 6) to support her decision and to deal with the impact it will have on the rest of the family.

A last word on turning: there may be information for the client in the opposite direction to the one they choose to begin with. At the end of the round, the invitation would be:

> *Now turn in the other direction until you know something else.*

Turning can also be helpful as an emergency measure if the client is in a position where emotional trauma is recurring and it is difficult for them to progress with conventional questioning. Even a small move one way or another can help.

We have looked at questioning the client at A in three ways: *stationary*, *moving*, and *turning*: facilitating A to resolve the problem at B or to meet the needs of B. When might we choose to deal with B directly? Can a problem be prompted to resolve itself?

§

Part Four Creating the Network

Chapter 3
What The Problem Knows

I am never afraid of what I know.   Anna Sewell
Let the malady speak.   Anon

One of the principal things Emergent Knowledge teaches us is the systems view. If A and B are components of an interconnected network, *A does not have to go to B* to get what it wants. Indeed, there is usually more than enough in the space between A and B to inhibit or prevent the client from taking the direct route, which is why the A → C → B relationship exists in the form that it does.

If A isn't lucky, good, or smart enough to get to B, can B be induced to bypass the usual rules and come to A? What happens if B becomes the subject rather than the object of the exercise? When a facilitator allows that *the system* knows, B may no longer be identified as the problem, but a potential source of the solution.

> *And what does that* [the statement at B] *know*? or

> *And what else could go on there* [the paper holding the statement]*?* or

> *And is there another place that could go?*

The voyagers who made their way across thousands of miles of featureless Pacific imagined their ocean-going canoes as the center of the universe and their island objective as coming to them through the benign agency of the wind and the waves. Just as the stars were seen to move across the night sky above, the sea could be conceived as slipping purposefully beneath, bringing the objective ever nearer. When a problem at B is viewed as a remote but integral part of an essentially benevolent system, what might seem like a perilous journey full of uncertainty is transformed.

QUESTIONING THE PROBLEM AT B

[Indicating statement at B] *And what does that know?*
[Of the response] *Put that down.*

And what else does that know?
[Repeat this question five times in all]

And now *what does that know?*

And now what do you *know?*

Alternatively [indicating statement/drawing at B]
And what else could go on there?
[Of the response] *Put that down.*

[Repeat question and invitation six times in all]

In an emergent system, information has value whatever its source. Questioning B is like gearing the search engine into overdrive. When there is less pressure on the vehicle to respond, less fuel is consumed. The client at A continues to do the work, but indirectly.

If you find yourself thinking that a problem could hardly be expected to know much about itself, try asking it. And invite the client to record their responses ("Put that down"), because what happens at B may be unusual or surprising, and recording what happens will make the changes explicit.

B does not have to remain in one place, by the way. The client at A can be asked whether B would like to move physically in the same way that A itself can be asked:

Is there another place that [statement or drawing] *could go /would like to be?*

A different perspective generates new information.

And what does it/that know from there?

And so on. Grove adapted the technique of questioning B for the Paris salon ("And what else could go on there?").

In the box, 'Questioning the Problem at B' (page 147), you will have noticed *two* learning questions after the iterative six.

*And now what does **that** know?*

refers to the subject of the round, the statement at B, to which the standard six questions were addressed. The learning should always return to the client, however:

*And now what do **you** know?*

Ensuring that the lesson is embodied, and thus *known* to be known.

ZAK is a builder's laborer who has reluctantly agreed to be referred for psychotherapy. He enters the consulting room with his left hand and arm heavily bandaged. His first words to me are:

I don't know why I'm here.
[I indicate paper and pens] *Put that down.*
What?
Put down, "I don't know why I'm here."

Zak looks hard at me for a moment, then grabs a piece of paper and scrawls in large letters:

"I WAS SO ANGRY I PUT MY FIST THROUGH THE DOOR."
                                                    [#1 proclaim]

[I nod towards the paper] *And what else does that know?*

Zak looks at what he has written.

The door was the nearest thing.   [#2 explain]
Put that down.
(He does so, reluctantly)

And what else does that know?
I was justified!   [#3 reinforce]
Put that down ... And what else does that know?

It doesn't know what possible good all this is gonna do.
[#4 the wobble]

I nod at the paper. Zak puts down a version of what he has said. He has already filled two sheets of flipchart paper. I plough on.

And what else does that know?

Zak's face crumples suddenly. He surprises me by crawling under a table and taking the papers with him. It is as if A, B, and C together are exploring the recovered information space of D.

I can't be angry here.   [#5 crash and burn]
Put that down ...

And what else does that know?
I'm not angry, I'm scared.   [#6 out of the ashes]
Put that down.

(I nod towards Zak's papers) *And* now *what does that know?*
My dad had a big leather belt he used to thrash me with.
[learning]

Zak shakes his head and takes a deep breath. This is unexpected.

And now what do you *know?*
I'm no better than my dad.   [learning]

He stares at the paper. He tells me he has never made a connection between his father's violence and his own before. Not all clients will reveal so much about themselves *to* themselves in so short a time, but it happens enough not to be extraordinary. I ask Zak what he wants now.

To go home. No, go on. I might as well.

"Look into the depths of your own soul and learn first to know yourself," said Freud, "then you will understand why this illness was bound to come upon you." Still true, though you don't have to spend years in analysis to look into the depths and know yourself. The illness may speak, even if the client cannot.

§

Part Four Creating the Network

Chapter 4

What The Space Between Knows

Dare to know! Immanuel Kant

The space between the client at A and the problem at B, normally never acknowledged, let alone examined, is the typically tight-lipped link to which we give the sobriquet of 'C'.

QUESTIONING THE SPACE OF C

*A*nd *what does* [nod to C] *the space between know?*

And what else does it/that/the space know?
[Repeat this question five times in all]

And now *what does it/that/the space know?*

And now what do you *know?*

NEIL is a likeable young man who has been having problems with a succession of girlfriends. He wants to settle down, he says, but has been unable to sustain a relationship for longer than a month or two. David has questioned Neil at A and his statement at B, and has invited him to write up what he knows about what he has learned ("I need to find myself before I can be with another person") as homework.

Neil comes in for second session. He has a serious expression and a drawing of what he describes as his "brain", which he tacks to the inside of the consulting room door. His first words today are:

Something's happened to my brain. At the start when I
came, it was messy and numb. Now it's awakening and
stimulated, but ...

He goes quiet and moves to the other side of the consulting room.
David nods to the space between Neil and his "brain".

And what does that space know?
That there's a wall between us.   [#1 proclaim]

And what else does that know?
On this side, it knows this is the way for you to go. And
on the other is what you want to leave.   [#2 explain]

And what else does that know?
That it's not too clever, but it's strong.   [#3 reinforce]

The space of C is likely to hold information about what is keeping
A from resolving B, or, in Neil's case, from finding himself before
he can be with another person.

And what else does that know?
That it's not ... well, it has a strange door, it's looking at me.
                                                   [#4 the wobble]

And what else does that know?
That the door is too hot to touch.   [#5 crash and burn]

And what else does that know?
The door is opening itself a bit.   [#6 out of the ashes]

And now *what do* you *know?*

David has omitted, "And now what does *that* know?", which could
be an oversight or a deliberate shortcut. When questioning B, I
recommend you include it as a matter of course (before "And now
what do *you* know?"). Neil responds:

To pull all the things I want to take with me through the
door and leave the rest behind the wall.   [learning]

As often as not, the information in the unfamiliar environment of
C will appear in symbolic form. As the client gets to know more

about C and its symbols, the metaphor is likely to modify. Neil discovers a "wall" between him and his brain [#1]. As he describes the wall [#1, #2, and #3], "a strange door" appears in it [#4]. The door becomes "too hot to touch" [#5], but then [at #6] it begins "opening itself a bit." Just as in a standard Therapeutic Metaphor or Symbolic Modeling process, as the metaphor transforms, the underlying problem the metaphor represents begins to resolve.

What prompts Neil and his unconscious to take certain things "through the door" and to leave the rest "behind the wall"? We can speculate forever, but it is not our direct concern. The client is in the throes of a process that only he and his unconscious control, and while we may wonder about the meaning of his metaphor, our job is to help it resolve in the way that it will.

We have worked with *the client at A* (stationary, moving, and turning); with *the problem at B* (stationary and moving, though B is perfectly capable of turning too); and with *the space between of C*. There is another way.

§

Part Four Creating the Network

Chapter 5
What The System Knows

The unexamined life is not worth living. Socrates

Here are two ways of treating the A B C system the client has created *as a unit*. NICOLA is asked to view her problem and herself from an observer position outside the system; there are elements here of NLP's 'meta-mirror' exercise. CORINNE, in a more experimental process, is invited to manipulate the three parts of her system together.

NICOLA is a 33-year old software designer who runs her own business. She lives with the man she fell in love with ten years ago and they have a nine-month old baby girl. At the start of her first session, Nicola tells me that her work is going well, her relationship with her partner is good, the baby is thriving, she feels well supported by family and friends, and yet she is deeply depressed.

During several sessions working with a variety of Clean Space, Intergenerational Healing, and Power of Six processes, Nicola has admitted to herself that she is not finding her work as creative and fulfilling as it used to be; that there are underlying problems in her relationship with her partner, including arguments over bringing up the baby; and that she feels emotionally remote from her mother. Unwrapping this bundle of feelings is helping her feel less depressed, but now she is puzzled:

> Why am I so confused? Why is it so hard for me just to let
> go and feel positive and excited again?

Nicola has traded depression for confusion, which I take to be some kind of improvement. I invite her to write up these questions to herself and to place the paper in spatial relationship to every other statement and drawing she has made since she first came. She arranges the papers on the floor and I take her through a standard Clean Start, which sets up an A B C threesome in which Nicola is at A, her papers are at B, and there is a space of C between her and the papers. I indicate the lot, including Nicola herself:

Find a space that knows about all that.

This might have to be clarified. What we are seeking is a 'meta-position' that is *not* the one the client had taken up as a result of the Clean Start.

QUESTIONING A B C

Find a space that knows about all that.

And what does all that know?

And what else does it/all that know?
[Repeat the question five times in all]

And now *what does it/all that know?*

And now what do you *know?*

Nicola finds what she calls an "observer" position standing on a chair, where, she says, "I see everything clearly."

And what does all that know?
Hm. It's like a snapshot of my life and a snapshot of my parent's life.   [#1 proclaim]

And what else does all that know?
It knows I've learned a lot, but I'm still confused.
                                                     [#2 explain]

And what else does all that know?
That I feel a bit better, but I'm not sure if it's for the right
reasons.   [#3 reinforce]

She smiles weakly. I guess she is acknowledging the bind she is in.
If she thought that she were feeling better for the wrong reasons,
would she still be feeling better?

And what else does all that know?
I know it doesn't matter what the reasons are, but ... well, I
know there are things about my Mum I should find out
more about. That I should do rather than I want to do.
                                          [#4 the wobble]

And what else does all that know?
I can never let go, get high with my friends. But why should
I have to be like that? Being on the fringe looking in is okay,
isn't it? I'd like to completely let go, no matter what, and I
can't.   [#5 crash & burn]

And what else does all that know?
Maybe I'm getting carried away. Maybe having just a bit of
fun will be enough.   [#6 out of the ashes]

And now *what do* you *know?*
I should make sure I do the things that allow me to have fun.
                                          [learning]

The learning leads to an action plan in which Nicola aims to make
more time to talk with her partner, to find out more about her
mother, and to find ways of doing more of the kind of work she
finds fulfilling and less of the kind she does not. Her process
continues.

CORINNE is a therapist in her sixties who has been trying to come
to terms over the years with her existential struggle to find
meaning at a very deep level. She tells David and me that she has
not yet reached a place in her process where she feels able to say,
"That's it." Not surprisingly, perhaps, because what she wants is
"To understand my place in an unfathomable universe." Anything
unfathomable is by definition incapable of being fully understood,
which is, I suppose, as good a reason as any for trying.

David has found an old clothes dryer, which we rig up as a kind of rack on wheels with a sheet of cartridge paper attached to one side. Wheels are useful for an exercise like this, but not essential. A flipchart stand can be moved. A cardboard box with the client's statement taped to it can be moved. Paper itself can be moved.

Corinne has the use of a large, empty loft, but a client's internal sense of space will adjust to whatever physical space is available. If a client needs to extend their horizons, there are always other spaces. I have worked with people in the kitchen, in the cellar, on the stairs, in the garden and the local park, in all weathers. One client discovered that the 'adjacent' spaces he needed were in the street outside. He stood there for an hour or more, oblivious to the cold, while David and I took it in turns to supply him with questions and the occasional mug of tea.

Seeing the loft and the clothes dryer, Corinne asks:

> Where do I start?
> *There.* [David indicates the paper] *Put that up there.*
> (Corinne writes on the paper) "WHERE DO I START?"

Exactly where Corinne starts does not matter, of course. She knows she can start anywhere. Whatever a client first proclaims will have meaning at some level. The emergent process will itself do the rest.

David guides Corinne through a standard Clean Start, which ends with her statement on the rig five or six meters away and Corinne facing it defiantly, feet apart, arms akimbo, as if it were a willful adversary. It will be some months before I discover what the statement actually represents for Corinne.

Referring to the system as a complete entity – Corinne at A, her statement on the rig at B, and the space between them at C – David asks:

> *And what does all that know?*
> It knows something, but I don't.   [#1 proclaim]
> *Is there another space it can move to?*

He could equally have said, "Move it where it needs to be." There are similarities here to working solely with B, but differences too. The client is not being asked to direct their attention to any one part of the self-system, but to the system as a whole. This presupposes a situation in which the client is already familiar with A, B, and C separately.

MOVING A B C

And what does it/all that know?

Is there another space it/all that can move to?
[Or] *Move it/all that where it needs to be.*

And what does it/all that know there?

[Repeat invitation and question six times in all]

And now *what does it/all that know?*

And now what do you *know?*

Is there another space it can move to?

David could have continued with "all that" instead of "it", but he has picked up on Corinne's first response: "*It* knows something, but I don't." Her "it" could be a reference to the rig, or to the paper, or to what either or both represent for her. David's ambiguous "it" can therefore be taken by Corinne to refer to the knowledge that the space of B possesses, or to what the statement at B holds, or to information in C, or to A B C as a whole.

Our present-day sense of 'ambiguous' derives from the Old French *ambigu*, 'a banquet at which a medley of dishes is set upon together.' Offered a feast of possible meanings, the client will make an instinctive decision about which dish they prefer without too much thought.

Corinne moves the rig, stops it, and moves to a new position relative to it.

> *And what does it know there?*
> It doesn't like that. It's a bit orderly.   [#2 explain]

Again, we can only guess at what Corinne's "that" might be and whether her second "it" is the same or different from the first. In a Clean Language procedure, we would expect to separate out these its and thats and get the client to define them. There is no need to do that here. The important thing is that the client herself knows what she means. David continues:

> *Is there another space it can move to?*

Corinne moves herself and the rig a quarter-turn and takes it further away from us.

> *And what does it know there?*
> It knows more about something there, but I don't.
> > [# 3 reinforce]

Here is a search pattern applied to a system that is not fixed, as was Nicola's, but fluid. The facilitator has no need to know what the problem is, or the meaning or significance of the moves that the client makes, even though the facilitator (and the moves) may be very curious indeed. All David has to do is keep count and stay out of the way, not as easy as it sounds when the session is an extended one and the whole space is psychoactive. I observe my colleague, who could dominate any space he chose, edging gently round the perimeter of the loft like a mild-mannered coach on the sidelines, unwilling to enter the field of play.

> *Is there another space it can move to?*

Corinne wheels the rig to the far side of the loft and turns it until the question to herself ("Where do I start?") is facing away from her. The whole A B C dynamic has changed.

> *And what does it know there?*
> Well, it knows it doesn't want other people to know.
> > [#4 the wobble]

> *Is there another space it can move to?*

The client gives the rig a slight nudge. It hardly moves.

> *And what does it know there?*

Corinne does not answer for a while, then:

>That it's an unanswerable question.   [#5 crash and burn]

Another move, a very slight one.

>*And what does it know there?*
>That it's a very central question.   [#6 out of the ashes]

>*And* now *what does it know?*
>That it's resistant to change. (She clenches her teeth).
>   [learning #1]

>*Put that on there.*

Under "WHERE DO I START?" Corinne writes:

RESISTANT
TO CHANGE

Corinne's first learning

Client and rig are taken through a second round in which the problem persists. At the end:

>*And* now *what do* you *know?*
>That it's still resistant.   [learning #2]
>*Put that on there.*

Corinne grits her teeth again and before "RESISTANT" inserts:

VERY

Second learning

Client and facilitator persevere through a third round in which Corinne learns that no matter what happens, no matter how much she changes the component parts of her system by rearranging the spatial and positional relationships of A to B, B to A, A to C, and so on, the question she posed at the start remains unanswered. "Where do I start?" continues to be "Very resistant to change." Nothing has shifted.

At the end of the round, Corinne says quietly, almost bitterly:

> It's teaching me at least what I do with the question, how
> I struggle with it.   [learning #3]

In Round Four, Corinne moves herself and the rig around the loft with renewed determination. David stays with her, remains unobtrusive, and concentrates on his timing. My job as co-facilitator in an extended session like this is to be a witness, take notes, prompt David as necessary, and be ready to take over.

At the end of the round, Corinne reports:

> The problem diminishes when I don't focus on it. Although
> it has a powerful desire to be central, it is not always
> central. I can push it away. (Pushes the rig away and lets it
> run.) I know that I can be in a position of power and it is
> losing its grip.   [learning #4]

Throughout Rounds Five and Six, Corinne remains in a symbiotic relationship to the rig, covering all the available space: pushing, pulling, and turning the rig; placing herself at various distances and angles to it; standing, sitting, even lying on the floor. Meanwhile she has a series of revelations about "Very resistant to change:"

> It is struggling with itself.
> I quite like the fact that it is struggling with itself.
> It can only be powerful if I let it.
> I feel quite empowered by it. If it is to be, it's up to me.
> I have to be open to doing things differently.
> I don't have to clench my teeth.
> Then I feel softer and more peaceful.
> Then things will work out in their own way.
> The universe gets on with its business.
> It is a caring, benevolent universe.
> It cares for me.   [learnings #5 and #6]

There is no acknowledgment from the client that her problem has transformed or modified in any significant way, but it has been rigorously tested and she has found a way of dealing with it. She is no longer confined to the small world in which she began ("It knows something, but I don't"). She has explored its boundaries and limitations fully and journeyed beyond it to the "caring, benevolent universe" of which it is a mere part. Some months later, I learn from Corinne that although she had been in remission from cancer for many years, it had recently returned. Her cancer was the "it" on which she had been working.

Many, if not most, therapists would be dismayed not to have information like this up-front so that they could get on with a self-imposed task of 'helping the client come to terms with it.' Yet this is Corinne's condition, she has chosen to work on it in this way, and now she is living with it in the context of a caring, benevolent universe. The seeds of healing of a kind have been sown. Twelve months later, Corinne comments:

> I remember hating that damn clothes dryer with a vengeance and pushing it about really made me mad! But I know now it was about the struggle not to let the cancer be central in my life. I had to find a way not to be consumed by it. I find it amazing to read my struggle to find a place for the cancer in my life – so that it has a *place* in my life, but is *not* my life.
>
> I see this piece of work as being part of my search for answers to existence and how to place my cancer in that. And there are no answers. But I came to a place of peace in the work and a letting go. It has been an incredible experience reading this. Thank you. I feel reaffirmed.

Every case history in this book has been chosen to illustrate the structure of a particular Power of Six process, but the content that comes to light will always be unique, and some of it will touch the heart a little more than others.

In Chapters 1 to 5 of *Creating the Network* we witnessed an opening gambit (*A Clean Start*), three classic moves (*Questioning A, Questioning B*, and *Questioning C*), and one virtuoso maneuver (*Questioning the System*). Is there a typical end game?

§

Part Four Creating the Network

Chapter 6
Action Plan

There is no knowledge that is not power.   Ralph Waldo Emerson

Towards the end of a session, clients are invited to formulate a final search and discovery pattern for themselves. An 'Action Plan' is a bridge to tomorrow, a means by which the client can engage with the knowledge they have recovered, embody it physically and emotionally, and take more control of their lives.

> *Get another piece of paper. And knowing what you know now, construct an action plan. Six specific things you will do when you have left here. At least one of them you will do today. Not big things. Simple behaviorally based things. Maybe one or two to do tomorrow and the rest over the next week or so.*
>
> *What is it you are going to do?*
> *Where are you going to do it?*
> *When?*
> *And if with someone else, whom?*

The Action Plan is a client-generated list of behaviors aimed at consolidating and capitalizing on what has been learned during the session. The list should not be conceptual or general ("Be kind to myself," "Take more exercise," "Keep a diary."). The actions to be taken should be specific, observable, and repeatable. Compiling this list is not a task to be undertaken lightly or left to the last minute. It is integral to the work. The facilitator's task is to keep the client to the mark in making the plan and to ensure that each point on it is practical and material.

ACTION PLAN

*List six specific behavioral things you are
going to do to follow up what you have learned.*

*For each action, state:
what you are going to do
when you will do it
where
by yourself or with whom.*

At the age of ten, LENA was taken from an abusive birth family and placed with foster parents. Now aged twelve, "She has been having some problems with anger," according to her foster father. At first Lena refuses to talk to either David or me, but agrees to write and draw silently in response to our questioning. At the end of two rounds, David asks her:

So what's different for you now than when you first came in?

Lena speaks for the first time during the session:

I feel happier. (She smiles shyly)
Anything else?
Getting everything down, so it's gone.

A subtle insight. She is referring to her writing and drawing, her chosen way of 'getting things out there.'

What have you discovered from being here?
I know that things happen for a reason ... that it's part of life and it doesn't happen all the time ... and being bossed around at home makes me a bit annoyed!

I introduce Lena to the idea of listing six things she will do for herself as a result of what she has learned.

What are you going to call your plan?
(She writes) "THINGS I'LL DO!"

What's the first?
(Writes) "Go roller-blading."

When will you do that?
Friday afternoon.

With anyone or on your own?
With my sister.

And the next thing?

Lena gets the idea. She writes first, then explains:

"Play in the park." On Tuesday as long as it's not raining. If it is, then on Wednesday, with my sister or foster mother.

And the next?
"Color in a picture." Or draw some pictures, on Monday afternoon by myself.

Next?
"Go for a walk around the lake." Friday morning, with Dad and the dog.

Another?
"Play with my sister on the X-box."

And number six?
"Help out the family." Anything I'm told to do, like vacuuming.

Lena is sorting for significance, making ˌher own choices about what she will do as a result of 'news of difference.' In his book, *In Search of Memory*, social scientist Eric Kandel points out that voluntarily attending to and maintaining attention on what people *themselves* judge to be salient is a determining factor in converting information about change from short term to long term memory.

For twelve-year old Lena, the experience of making her own decisions about what is right for her marks a major change from being at the mercy of events to having control of them. There is not one suggestion on her list from the therapist and not one from her foster father. The more Lena refers to her personal plan and the more she performs the actions it names, the more important her brain will deem the newly activated neural pathways to be and the more likely her learnings ("It's part of life and doesn't happen all the time," etc.) are to last.

JAMIE is a 40-year old council worker who presents with a diagnosis of claustrophobia. At the end of his fourth round, he moves into action plan mode spontaneously:

> I'm the only person that stops me being free, that makes my neck and shoulders tense. I need to unlearn all those protect myself habits. The other day I cried for myself, the first time for ages. I can cry for others easily enough. It isn't too late to take the steps to be creative and joyful.
>
> *How many steps?*
> Probably seven – one new step each day.

I invite Jamie to list his seven steps. He lists six.

> *That's six. What happened to the seventh?*
> (He thinks carefully) I think six is enough. I'm exhausted.

David intervenes:

> *The best thing you can do is go home and have a good long sleep. Your body has all the information it needs. Your brain has to catch up. What did you come in for originally, by the way?*
> Erm ... (Jamie has some difficulty remembering)

§

In Part Four, we considered how to generate the basic components of an information network (*A Clean Start*); how to facilitate the component parts to create the network (*What the Client Knows, What the Problem Knows, What the Space Between Knows, What the System Knows*); and how to capitalize on the knowledge that emerges from the operation of the network (*The Action Plan*). Six search and discovery heuristics that make up the basic Power of Six algorithm. The pragmatist in Muhammed al-Gwarizmi would have approved, although the mathematician in him might have added, "I want to see more proofs."

Part Five

SIX DEGREES OF FREEDOM

1 In Everyday Life

2 In Personal Development

3 In Relationship

4 In Healing

5 In Problem Solving

6 In Business Development

When you know yourselves, then you will be known, but if you do not know yourselves, then you live in poverty.
Sayings of Jesus from the Gospel of Thomas

Avoidable human misery is more often caused not so much by stupidity as ignorance, particularly our ignorance about ourselves. Carl Sagan

Part Five Six Degrees of Freedom

Introduction

Knowledge comes through suffering.   Aeschylus, 'Agamemnon'

SANDRA	I need to lose weight.
SIMON	I'm in a mess. Having too many arguments. I've got to settle myself down and get some direction.
EVA	I'm in a relationship with a really nice guy, but I feel trapped, I'm stuck, I can't breathe.
MONIKA	I want my back pain to soothe and to get back my mobility.
ERIC	I don't want anythin'!
SILVIE	I need to generate more clients, but to do that I need more money and to get more money I need more clients.
JULIA	I want to explore the problems and possibilities of working with an American colleague in France.

NASA has developed a machine for training space pilots that can move longitudinally (forwards and backwards), vertically (up and down), and laterally (left and right) while rotating in three different ways (pitch, roll, and yaw). They call it 'Six Degrees of Freedom.' As a metaphor for mental and emotional flexibility, this would be freedom indeed.

The principles and practices of Emergent Self Knowledge and the Power of Six apply over a wide range of concerns and conditions. I have grouped these into six broad categories – *Everyday Life*, *Personal Development*, *Relationship*, *Healing*, *Problem Solving*, and *Business* – though there are, of course, overlaps. A client for business development will almost certainly have related personal issues, as will a client with relationship difficulties or a physical symptom.

The examples here illustrate solutions to a variety of problems within these categories. They are taken from casework by David Grove and me working separately and together in London, Auckland, Normandy, and Paris. I began by selecting cases where the client's responses were in general quite short, thinking this would make them easier to follow on the page, but after analyzing a number of transcripts, I was reminded of the extent to which brevity, immediacy, and relevance are typical of the process (though there were honorable exceptions). This told me something about self-organization. The precision and predictability of the Power of Six questions do not in general produce extended exchanges. The questions concentrate the client's mind so that the course it follows is direct.

'Freedom' is a state of mind that most clients for change and healing pursue, consciously or not. It takes many forms. In Part Two, Cathy sought freedom from panic attacks, Ken from work-related stress, and Tina from her obsession with cleanliness. In Part Four, Marie sought freedom from depression, Lorraine from her aches and pains, Zak from the grip of family violence, Neil from his compulsive behavior, Nicola from a state of confusion, Corinne from existential angst, and Lena from anger and unhappiness.

Here now are stories of seven other clients seeking freedom of other kinds. SANDRA is desperate to lose weight, SIMON longs to get out of the "mess" his life is in, EVA is trapped in an unsuitable relationship, MONIKA wants peace from chronic back pain and ERIC from a childhood trauma, while SILVIE is in the throes of an identity crisis, and JULIA has a professional and personal dilemma she needs to resolve.

You will find a few differences here to the tales other therapists tell, as you might expect having come this far. I am less interested in chronicling a client's personal and family history, or in hallucinating what they might be thinking or feeling, or in speculating about their relationship with the therapist, than I am in recording *exactly what happens during the session*: who says what and what they do. We have seen how adept the Power of Six is at bringing sub-text to the surface. The inner life of these characters is revealed in what they say and how they are in the moment.

The dialogue in the transcripts, as elsewhere in the book, is taken from verbatim notes I made at the time, with one exception. Monika's is a special case in that her process involved writing down her own responses, and with her permission I have used these. Very little editing has been applied to any of the transcripts. Except where clients gave permission, identifying characteristics have been changed, though to no particular pattern. Some client responses, for example those I classify as 'wobbles' or 'crashes', may not always make the same sense on the page as they did in the live process, but most, I trust, will. The client learnings at the end of each round are in general quite clear.

In three cases (Sandra, Silvie, and Julia), emergent self knowledge became the basis for further work not reviewed here. In four other cases (Simon, Eva, Monika and Eric), I review their whole process. Between them, the seven cover the main search and discovery patterns introduced in Part Four: *A Clean Start*, *What the Client at A Knows*, *What the Problem at B Knows*, *What the Space of C Knows* and the *Action Plan*. These are cross-referenced in the form of sub-headings within the transcripts. I have not included another example of *What the System Knows*, as we looked at that in detail with Nicola and Corinne towards the end of Part Four.

One complete Clean Start (Simon's) is included as a reminder of its key role in every Power of Six process and of the way it integrates into the procedure as a whole. In all other cases, the client has been through a standard Clean Start to establish an A B C threesome before the transcript begins. *The full force of the Power of Six depends on the care given to this determination of the client's structural and spatial relationship to the problem.* It is an indispensable metaphor for what is going on internally.

In a good Clean Start, psychological shifts find their external equivalent and physical moves prompt internal shifts of perception. A client will move closer to their written or drawn analogue of the problem, for example, or change their angle to it as they get to know it better or as new knowledge takes the place of the old. The move confirms and furthers the internal shift. Change (or knowledge, or learning), sudden or incremental, emerges (Figure 31).

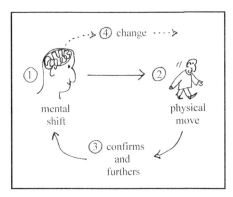

Figure 31. Mental shift expressed in physical move feeds back to mental.
Also happens the other way round: physical move prompts mental shift

Finally, a reminder that when every client process is unique, none of the cases here should be treated as typical. They demonstrate a few of the innumerable ways that the Power of Six can be applied, but they will, I trust, give you a sense of both its *predictability* and its *flexibility*. You will notice the odd variation from the standard questioning and response patterns laid down in Part Four: reality intervenes on occasion!

§

Part Five Six Degrees of Freedom

Chapter 1
In Everyday Life

A nimble six pence is better than a slow shilling.   English proverb

I shall not dwell too long in this category, as the possibilities are endless and the procedure speaks for itself. You can ask the six standard questions followed by the learning question of just about anyone in any context, though you might have to allow for a dusty answer or two if you were to try them out in the pub or at home. I would ask for a volunteer first.

Generally speaking, *Everyday Life* is a category that applies to two kinds of people: colleagues or friends who seem to be having some kind of minor existential problem and are happy to explore it in a slightly unusual way, and clients who begin conversationally or non-committally and you find yourself wondering, "Why are they telling me this? What might lie behind this?"

Two people who appeared in Part Two illustrate both. KEN is a friend who was anxious because he had too much going on in his life, and TINA is a client who came out with an innocent enough remark about cleaning the kitchen.

Ken's is an example of a round of six that was sufficient in itself at the time. His learning was, "There is space between things, I can make space."

Tina, on the other hand ("I am very fussy about cleaning") had me wondering, "Is there more to this?" From a relatively commonplace observation, she uncovered what might well have been a deeply sourced problem ("I am not much of a mother, but a critical person") and ended her first round with a clear cue

("I don't want them growing up like me") for a behavioral plan or for a second round of questioning. In fact, Tina went on for several more sessions and learned a lot more about the love and attention she had missed out on herself as a child, which helped her become more the mother she wanted to be.

SANDRA: I need to lose weight
What the client at A knows

We first met SANDRA ("I have a struggle with yo-yo dieting") in Part Three. She is a small, plump, cheerful woman in her forties. On the phone, she had spoken about wanting to talk about losing her father. When she arrives, she beams at me and says:

> I know, I know, I need to lose weight!   [#1 proclaim]
>
> *And what else do you know?*
> I've been overweight for eighteen years.   [#2 explain]
>
> *And what else do you know?*
> I've tried to lose weight a dozen times.   [#3 reinforce]
>
> *And what else do you know?*
> (She hesitates) I guess I don't know how.   [#4 the wobble]

The client is responding less readily than she was to begin with and is paying more attention to the information that appears. It is as if she has to drag the next response from deep within.

> *And what else do you know?*
> It's holding me back. There must be something in my subconscious mind, some reason why I'm holding on to this weight. (She looks very sad)   [#5 crash & burn]
>
> *And what else do you know?*
> I'm stuck.   [#6 out of the ashes]

Sandra is finally facing the reality of her situation.

> *And* now *what do you know?*
> I need to ... there is a way. I can't get to it.   [learning]

She goes on to articulate a desired outcome, "To feel better about myself," which she draws up and tacks to the wall. A second round of questioning leads her to finding out more about the "something" in her subconscious mind and to further work ("I start and stop and can never really get going") on self-image and her relationship with her late father.

Simple concerns are not always simple, so ask these simple questions with care. They can lead to other things.

§

Part Five Six Degrees of Freedom

Chapter 2

In Personal Development

*To be yourself in a world that is constantly trying to make
you something else is the greatest accomplishment.*
Ralph Waldo Emerson

SIMON: I'm in a mess
*A Clean Start, questioning A, questioning B, questioning C,
self-facilitating*

Simon is a painter and decorator in his late twenties who has been
referred to the outpatient clinic that Grove and I are running in
Auckland. I have chosen his process because it captures four
Power of Six patterns in one go: a Clean Start, questioning the
client at A, the problem at B, and the space between of C. It also
includes a creative variation on standard practice – not everything
reduces to a formula – and an illustration of the possibility of a
well-motivated client asking the questions of themself. The Power
of Six is an elitist model only in the sense that the client is the
expert, not the therapist. Simon quickly develops confidence in his
own expertise.

He walks in briskly, outgoing and curious. He can hardly wait to
tell us why he is here.

I'm in a mess. Having too many arguments. I've got to
settle myself down and get some direction.

SIMON: a Clean Start

David indicates papers and pens:

*Put that down. Then place it anywhere in the room it needs
to go and place yourself where you are now in relation to it.*

Without hesitation, Simon writes "I need to Sort my head out" on a large piece of paper, which he tacks to the back of the door. He goes to the far side of the room to consider it.

> I put it on the door because, well, it's the door – I'm like looking into some kind of movie.

> *Are you in the right space?*
> (Moves closer) Yeh.

> *Is that the right height?*
> No. (Places the statement a bit higher) Yeh.

Not unusually, the client has placed his objective a little above eye height.

> *Are you facing in the right direction?*
> (Tries various positions) Yeh. (Looks at the paper) It should be folded.
> *Fold it.*

Simon folds the paper in two with his statement inside. One could offer any number of interpretations of this, but the process will bring out what it needs to bring out for Simon himself. He replaces the paper on the back of the door.

> That's much better. Yeh, I feel better.
> *Is that at the right angle?*
> Yeh.

> *And are you at the right angle with respect to it?*
> Yeh.

> *Is that at the right distance?*
> (Simon moves, tests, ends up a bit closer) Yeh.
> *And is that the right distance?*

There is a difference between the last two questions. "Is that *at* the right distance?" refers to the paper at B. "Is *that* the right distance?" refers to the space between the client and the paper at B after the client has moved. It is one of the simple double checks built into the Clean Start procedure.

Simon moves back a little in response to "And is that the right distance?" He has changed his spatial relationship to the statement by a fraction only, but a little can go a long way and David is obliged to ask again:

> *Are you in the right space?*
> The thing about me is I'm very movable. At the cinema, I
> have to move two or three times before I get the right seat.
> (Looks at his paper) I think I need to change a few things.

> *Change what you need to change.*

Some facilitators would be impatient to get on with examining what Simon said when he first came in ("I'm in a mess. Having too many arguments"), but the ritual of a Clean Start is already doing that for Simon himself. He is finding out more about the mess he is in by the simple expedient of moving, adjusting, and readjusting position.

A Clean Start animates the information-rich psychoactivity of a session. How it does so will be different for each client and must take the time it takes. The facilitator should only embark on the next phase of questioning when the client has given affirmative responses to every question in the first phase.

Simon changes what he has been invited to change by tearing his statement in two and tacking one half (which he labels "I need to") on the wall, and the other half (labeled "Sort my head out" on the door. He steps back a couple of paces (Figure 32).

Figure 32. Simon says

The door signifies where I wanna be, the wall where I don't wanna be.

Simon is taken through a Clean Start for his relationship to each part in turn and a *further* Clean Start for his relationship to the two parts in tandem. There is meaning for the client in the way he has created this particular A B_1 B_2 C system and we must honor that. There may only be small differences to the positions that Simon finds during the process, but there will be information for him both *in* the difference and in his *seeking and finding* the difference.

After shifting this way and that in response to the Clean Start questions (the full list is on page 126), Simon finds a space that feels right for him. He can see both statements, but is noticeably nearer the door ("where I wanna be") than the wall ("where I don't wanna be").

SIMON round 1
What the problem at B knows

> *You have information. So does each of those* (David nods to the papers). *What does this one* (indicates 'sort my head out') *know?*
> It knows me – what I'm experiencing, feeling, the kind of person I am.
>
> *Put that on there.*
> Write it on?

Simon writes "me now" on the 'sort my head out' paper to the right and draws a little smiley ☺. I note that he has chosen to construct his response in the present rather than the future. Something may already be changing.

> *And what does this one* (indicating 'I need to') *know?*
> What does it know?

He writes "me past" on the 'I need to' paper to the left and returns to his original position.

> *And what do both know?*
> The same. Me and me past.   [#1 proclaim]

David gives an equivocal, almost imperceptible, nod to the papers as he continues to refer to them without specifying either or both:

And what else could go on there?

Simon looks at his 'I need to / me past' paper:

> It's pulling me.   [#2 explain]

> *And what else could go on there?*
> Leave me!

He writes "tears" and stands closer.   [#3 reinforce]

> *And what else could go on there?*

Simon frowns, hesitates, then moves to the 'Sort my head out / me now / ☺' paper, where he writes:

> I'm a good person.   [#4 the wobble]

> *And what else could go on there?*

He moves back to the 'me past' paper and writes, "sadness, madness, upset, I hate being here."   [#5 crash and burn]

> *And what else could go on there?*

On the right, he writes "friends".   [#6 out of the ashes]

Figure 33. Simon differentiates

And now *what do you know?*
I want all this (gestures to 'me past') to go away and I want
to be here ('me now'). Yep. Yep.   [learning #1]

So how are you doing?

One of David's interim questions. Simon grins, then frowns.

My head is sore.

He writes "sore head" on the right without prompting. It would be easy for a facilitator to ignore a casual aside like this, but Simon has already given it a form, and in any case, there are no casual asides on the Grovian stage. David acknowledges Simon's sore head with a standard Clean Language question:

> *Where is your head sore?*
> Everywhere. Head. Heart. I give grief to others.
>
> *For homework, find a space where you can write up a list of things. List the last things – your head is sore, your heart is sore, and you give grief to others – and list the different kinds of sore in your head, heart, and everywhere else, and list out the grief you give to others.*

David was never less than ambitious when it came to assignments. If a client managed to do a tenth of what he suggested, he would assume this to be the essential tenth. Simon does not wait to get home. He takes a black pen and starts to list his sores and griefs on the 'me past' paper; then with an orange pen writes in capitals on the 'me now' paper, "JOY, VISION, AMAZING EXPERIENCES."

> *List them out – the joy you give to others, the vision, the amazing experiences – who with, and what you did. So you're going to make two lists, in black and orange, and bring it all back next time.*

SIMON round 2
What the problem at B knows

Not many problems resolve after a single round, though some do. When Simon arrives for a second session, he is not quite as bouncy as when he appeared for the first. I expect him to be carrying reams of homework, but he brings nothing. He explains:

I want to have a clean slate.   [#1 proclaim]

David wastes no time commenting on the lack of homework or pursuing any notions of 'resistance'. He only has an idiosyncratic response to what the client has brought: the desire for "a clean slate."

> *Okay, put up a slate that isn't clean and write the things*
> *that don't want you to have a clean slate.*

Note the 'unclean' assumptions in this invitation – that there *is* a slate that isn't clean and that there *are* things that don't want Simon to have a clean slate. Even the cleanest of us cannot always be pristine. I include this intervention and the short sequence that follows because it happened that way. It tells you more about Grove and is a reminder that Clean and creative may sometimes sup at the same table.

Simon makes a long list of the things that do not want him to have a clean slate. He weeps silently as he does so.

> My life is crap.   [#2 explain]
> *Put up the tears.*

Simon draws (it so happens) six buckets. He explains:

> Buckets of tears ...   [#3 reinforce]
> *There's information in the tears.*

David makes a stage aside to me that Simon can hear:

> *Looks like all the crap is contained in those six buckets.*
> (Simon smiles) If it all goes in those, I can have a clean
> slate.

He bucks up a little and continues drawing and writing. David takes the opportunity to slip away to see another patient. I wait for Simon to complete his list and then continue. I abide by the formula:

And what else does that know?
There's far too much for six buckets.   [#4 the wobble]

And what else does that know?
I'm sick of shoveling all this shit in my life. [#5 crash and burn]

And what else does that know?
Something has to change and I guess it's me.
                                        [#6 out of the ashes]

Simon puts up his 'slate' on the 'me past' side of the door and studies it.

And now *what does that know?*
It can see what's going on. It's very clear.

And now what do you *know?*
I need to improve, find myself, further myself before I can
be where I wanna be. My energy needs to shine and then I
won't get sore, I'll be cool.   [learning #2]

He looks surprised at himself and ponders what he has just said. At that moment, the practice doctor puts her head round the door and asks if I can see another patient. I brief Simon to take himself through another round:

Now ask yourself the question "And what else do I know?"
six times and write up your responses. I'll be back soon.

SIMON round 3
Self-facilitation: what the client at A knows

I return a little while later to find Simon intently contemplating what he has written.

And now *what do you know?*
What I know is I need to change things, find myself. Yeh.
When you write it up and look at it ... I want it all to change.
                                        [learning #3]
Put that up.
I did already.

Simon shows me his list. David returns. Offstage, I have had the temerity to suggest that he refrains from freelancing around the formula with remarks like, "Put up a slate that isn't clean." This must have been like asking Marlon Brando to stick to the script in *Apocalypse Now*. A clear invitation to do something different.

SIMON round 4
What the client turning at A knows

David notices that Simon is seated on a swivel chair.

> *Turn your chair in either direction and when you know*
> *something, stop.*
> (Simon swivels a quarter turn to his left.)
>
> *What do you know from that direction?*
> Something new.   [#1 proclaim]
>
> *Another turn ... What do you know from that direction?*
> Something sounds warm.   [#2 explain]

What neuroscientists call a 'synesthesia'. Simon's auditory and kinesthetic signals have fused ("sounds warm") as the result of a moment of heightened connectivity in the brain. This could be a good thing or a bad thing. Is Simon signaling some kind of integration or is he confused?

> *Another turn ... What do you know from that direction?*
> I see light.   [#3 reinforce]

Now vision gets in on the act. As the new information comes in at number Three, I speculate that the warmth Simon heard and the light he saw were more likely to be self-reinforcing than contradictory. The client is staring ahead. After a momentary pause, David invites him to:

> *Keep turning ... What do you know from that direction?*
> Mm. (Frowns. Low, soft voice.) A barrier.   [#4 the wobble]

Turbulence. Just as land was in sight, a reef has appeared.

> *Another turn ... What do you know from that direction?*
> My head aches.   [#5 crash and burn]
>
> *Another turn ... What do you know from that direction?*
> (A change of tone) Hm. Creativity.   [#6 out of the ashes]

Simon has found a way through to warmer waters.

> *And* now *what do you know?*
> I feel smarter. A bit smarter. And comfortable.
> Everything falls into place, doesn't it?   [learning #4]

The wayfinder can drop anchor for a while.

It is obviously tempting to end a session with the client feeling smarter and comfortable and everything falling into place, but Simon shows no sign of wanting to go home. David offers him another prescription.

SIMON round 5
Self-facilitation: what the client turning at A knows

> *Keep turning until you feel a difference in what you know and at each point of difference ask yourself the question, "What else do I know?" Do this six times over and each time write up your response. We'll be back.*

Simon is keen to get on with the exercise and hardly notices us leaving. I look in after ten minutes or so to find him turning in his chair a little at a time, stopping, thinking, and writing. He nods at me, deep in thought. After a few moments, I ask quietly:

> *And* now *what do you know?*
> Things are very close to the surface. Who I am and who
> I want to be are quite – very – close. Yeh.   [learning #5]

SIMON round 6
What the space of C knows

David reappears. Simon explains:

> Something's happened to me. I'm turning, that's good, but something's stopping me. A force field between me and who I can be. A force field that says no.   [#1 proclaim]

If the space of C has information about what prevents the client at A from reaching B, as I proposed in Part Three, it could hardly be more clearly articulated than here: "Something's stopping me," proclaims Simon. "A force field between me and who I can be. A force field that says no." He has answered the question, "And what does the space between know?" for himself. All David has to do now is follow the path that Simon has set.

> *And what else does it know?*
> It's saying it's only a force field. It's there to get rid of
> things I don't want.   [#2 explain]

Simon is reporting what *the force field itself* is saying. The space of C is giving up its information directly.

> *And what else does it know?*

The client can take the ambiguous "it" to refer either to the force field or to anything else that he perceives as coming between him and who he can be. If the stimulus – the facilitator's question – is unchanging, the response will feed back on itself so that the new information will always be self-consistent.

Simon's response is:

> To focus. To work hard at what I want and the other things
> will disappear.   [#3 reinforce]
>
> *And what else does it know?*
> Is there a force field to be put up or taken down?
>   [#4 the wobble]
>
> *And what else does it know?*
> (Sighs) You're tired of force fields. Yeh.   [#5 crash and burn]

David looks to me and raises his eyebrows, a signal that he has lost count. He has been distracted by what Simon has been saying and has taken his eye off the ball. Easily done. Perhaps we should use coins or pebbles or whatever it is that cricket umpires pass from one pocket to another while counting the number of balls in an over. I come in with number six:

> *And what else does it know?*
> Force field knows there should be no force field.
>   [#6 out of the ashes]

And now *what does it know?*
Jesus, it's quite clear. Take action on myself and become
one person.   [learning #6]

I have asked the learning question ("And now what does *it*
know?") of the information in C to which David's earlier questions
had been addressed. If the problem at B had been the subject of the
questioning, I would have been obliged to ask the learning
question of B. In either case, the learning returns to the client:

And now what do you *know?*
That it's gonna be done. Fantastic! (Relaxes noticeably)
I feel quite smart.   [learning #6]

There may well be overlaps between the two kinds of learning
(what "it" knows and what "you" know), but that will only serve
to underline the lesson. And if, as with Simon, new information
appears ("it's gonna be done"), that cannot be bad. Finally, I ask:

And what is the difference between what you knew at the
start and what you know now?
The difference is I can become who I am.

The session ends with Simon's attention back on himself and his
ownership of the new information. He screws up all his papers and
grins at us wearily.

Wow. I'm tired.

It has been a long afternoon. David advises Simon:

Sleep on it. You've been working with your short-term
memory. Your long-term memory has to catch up.

Psychologists have been telling us for years about the importance
of sleep in learning and memory consolidation. The latest research
we have shows that a nap can provide as much benefit as a full
night.

§

Part Five Six Degrees of Freedom

Chapter 3
In Relationship

The field cannot well be seen from within the field.
Ralph Waldo Emerson

EVA: I feel trapped
What the problem at B knows, what the client at A/B knows

Eva is 32, a personal assistant in a media company. She is a lively young woman, quick to respond. At the age of four, Eva was taken by her parents from Poland to the USA. She remembers being happy in the States until the age of twelve or so, when the family moved to England and she was bullied at school. During her twenties, Eva had several close relationships with men that ended in mutual recrimination. She is confused at finding the pattern repeating.

Here is a client who responds as readily in writing and drawing as she does in speech. One reinforces the others and Eva, like Simon, is soon taking charge of her own process. You will notice her making intuitive use of color as she writes and draws. And there is a moment when she moves from the protagonist space of A directly into the problem space of B and stays there. Only at the last moment will she find release.

I have asked Eva to bring a representation of how things are for her now. She produces a sheet of paper with a drawing of a figure trapped in a transparent box, set in a landscape with undulating shapes going off into the distance. The picture has been drawn with a black pen. Eva ends her Clean Start with this drawing fixed just below eye level on the wall and herself only a step or two away. (Figure 34).

Figure 34. Eva now

Eva's physical proximity to the drawing may have something to say about her highly charged involvement with the metaphor.

EVA round 1 (black)
What the problem at B knows

> *What does that know here and now?*
> It knows I'm in a relationship with a really nice guy, but
> I feel trapped, I'm stuck, I can't breathe.   [#1 proclaim]
> *Put that on there.*

She chooses a black pen and writes on the drawing, "TRAPPED, STUCK," and steps back.

> *And what else does that know?*
> It isn't right for me, but I can't bring myself to tell him
> for fear of hurting him.   [#2 explain]

> *Put that on there.*
> (She writes "CAN'T TELL HIM" and steps back again)

My questions are addressed to and about the problem, but Eva is answering for herself, another likely indicator of the extent of her identification with the problem. No wonder she feels trapped.

> *And what else does that know?*
> There are opportunities, but I can't escape.   [#3 reinforce]

Eva now writes "OPPORTUNITIES" on the horizon of her drawing and "ESCAPE" to the right (Figure 35). This time she stays even closer to the drawing, only inches away.

Figure 35. Eva: "There are opportunities, but I can't escape"

Ad what else does that know?
Guilt. Fear. Pressure. Alone. Misunderstood. [#4 the
wobble]

Eva is now writing readily and rapidly as she speaks.

And what else does that know?
I feel empty. I don't feel myself. I'm confused.
(She sniffles. Tears begin to run down her cheeks)
[#5 crash and burn]

And what else does that know?
I <u>can</u> do <u>more!</u> I can <u>fulfill</u> things!   [#6 out of the ashes]

And now *what does that know?*
That I know why I'm like this.

And now *what do* you *know?*
(She shakes her head) But I don't really know.
[learning #1]

A pause as Eva looks at what she has written: "I know why I'm
like this, but don't really know." Learning of a sort, I suppose.

EVA round 2 (brown)
What the client at A/B knows

After a moment I ask:

And what else do you know?

Eva picks out a brown pen and writes as she speaks:

Insecure. [#1 proclaim]

She is writing practically everything she says now, so although my questions are addressed directly to the client at A, somehow they manage to address themselves to the problem at B as well.

> *And what else do you know?*
> I have to break the cycle because it is hurting me.
> [#2 explain]
> *And what else do you know?*
> I recognize it is very unhealthy. [#3 reinforce]
>
> *And what else do you know?*
> It seems I've convinced myself that I don't deserve to
> be happy. [#4 the wobble]
>
> *And what else do you know?*
> If I don't solve it I'm going to be alone ... forever ... no
> friends, the wrong relationships, I'll never be happy.
> [#5 crash and burn]
> *And what else do you know?*
> Guilt is stopping me from breaking this cycle
> relationship-wise. [#6 out of the ashes]

This time she writes the word "GUILT" on her drawing.

> *And* now *what do you know?*
> I'm desperate. I need to sort something out as soon
> as possible. [learning #2]

We continue without a pause.

EVA round 3 (green)
What the client at A/B knows

> *And what else do you know?*
> I'm a bit of a coward. [#1 proclaim]

She writes "COWARD" in green, underlines it: "COWARD". She is on a roll. I have only to keep count.

> *And what else do you know?*

I'm carrying on with a relationship that's not right.

[#2 explain]

And what else do you know?
More guilt (underlines the word "GUILT" in green) –
I don't want to hurt this person who I care about a lot.

[#3 reinforce]

Figure 36. What Eva knows

And what else do you know?
My parents ... traditional Polish Catholics ... I feel pressure
to marry him and settle down.   [#4 the wobble]

And what else do you know?
A fear of getting old. I behave in a very childish way
sometimes. I'm immature, and I'm thirty-two years old.

[#5 crash and burn]

And what else do you know?
I guess people, men, misunderstand me.   [#6 out of the ashes]

And now what do you know?
It almost seems like I'm doing it intentionally, just to push
them away.   [learning #3]

Eva is processing quickly and her writing is just keeping up.
Occasionally she paraphrases.

EVA round 4 (blue)
What the client at A/B knows

> *And what else do you know?*

Eva chooses a new, blue, pen, writes "I LET THEM IN, THEN SHUT THEM OUT."

> I let them in and then when I feel they get too close,
> I completely shut them out.   [#1 proclaim]
>
> *And what else do you know?*
> I feel they won't <u>like me</u>.   [#2 explain]
>
> *And what else do you know?*
> They see me as insensitive, cruel, arrogant, a tease –
> untrustworthy, unstable.   [#3 reinforce]
>
> *And what else do you know?*
> I don't want them to see this. I'm not like this.
>   [#4 the wobble]
> *And what else do you know?*
> Then I get frustrated. I'm in tears.   [#5 crash and burn]
>
> *And what else do you know?*
> I want to know why I do this. I know that I'm scared,
> but I want to know how I can <u>stop</u>.   [#6 out of the ashes]
>
> *And* now *what do you know?*
> I know I can stop it. I need to learn to accept myself first.
>   [learning #4]

The flip charts are filling up.

EVA round 5 (red)
What the client at A/B knows

> *And what else do you know?*
> (Surprised at her own response) I need to realize that I am
> who I am!   [#1 proclaim]

She finds a red pen and writes, "I AM WHO I AM" very clearly.

> *And what else do you know?*

> Some of these people who misunderstand me don't really
> give me a chance.   [#2 explain]

Eva has widened her frame of reference from her boyfriend to
people in general and from being at odds in one relationship to
difficulties with others. She continues, still using the red pen:

> Then I ask myself, are they really worth knowing to
> begin with?   *[# 3 reinforce]*

An example of a 'missed' question. I suppose that in the pause
after her second response, Eva has asked an intuitive "And what
else do I know?" of herself.

> *And what else do you know?*
> Sometimes I'm hard on myself. I'm too concerned with
> what others think.   [#4 the wobble]

> *And what else do you know?*
> I shouldn't be really! Why do I forget this?! [#5 crash and burn]

> *And what else do you know?*
> That's it.   [#6 out of the ashes]

Eva looks intently at everything she has written, then launches off
without the least prompting from me and answers what would
have been the 'learning' question for herself.

> I need to learn to remember this always.

The question was in the air, but invisible. There may well be
something intrinsic to the 6 + 1 exploration and consolidation
pattern (see *After Six, or One Revisited* in Part Two). Eva
continues:

> Not forget myself. I am who I am and I can't be someone
> else.   *[learning #5]*

EVA round 6 (red)
What the client at A/B knows

> Yes, this is it.

She writes furiously, keeping the same color for the first time as she works her way through a sixth round without a single intervention from me. The breakdown below is my retrospective analysis.

I've always tried pleasing people in the past .. *[#1 proclaim]*

even in school, trying to please the crowd, trying to fit in ...
[#2 explain]

trying to please parents ...   *[#3 reinforce]*

weight was always an issue with them ... trying to be thin, pretty, fashionable ...   *[#4 the wobble]*

because of all this trying to please in the past, I've just gotten so fed up that I've completely given up on pleasing now. It hasn't worked, trying to please, hence I'm just giving up pleasing. They weren't pleased. I've been let down ... my parents are still critical – I'm never good enough ... there was always something.
[#5 crash and burn]

I've just tried too hard ... too much concentrating importance on something that was just not worth it.
[#6 out of the ashes]

She steps back from the flipchart for the first time since the first round. There is a long pause as she contemplates everything she has written. Eventually:

That's it. That really is it.   *[learning #6]*

She steps further away from the paper. There is a finality to her voice and a new, relaxed manner. She is breathing more easily.

And what is the difference between what you knew at the start and what you know now?

She looks at me for the first time in a while.

Complete. I'm not trapped. I can say what I think. I know it's okay to be myself.   [difference]

Eva takes a few strides around the room as if to exercise her newly found freedom, smiles to herself, smiles at me, and returns to her chair.

EVA's Action Plan

Eva has no difficulty thinking what she needs to do next. I only have to prompt her now and again about when and where she will do it.

> 1 Stop being so hard on myself – remind myself I am who I am. Every day starting at 6 a.m. while jogging and again when I've finished.
>
> 2 Think about what I want to say to my partner. On my way home today. Arrange to talk over lunch.
>
> 3 Talk to him. Be honest with him. Tell him I don't think it's gonna work out.
>
> 4 Suggest to him we follow up and arrange another time to talk again.

She leaves the outcome of her negotiation with her partner open, which seems in principle a good idea. With the next note, there is a distinct change:

> 5 Speak to my boss. This P.A. job is just not me. I can offer a lot more. First thing tomorrow, I'll look at his calendar and write myself into it. I need to discuss my future. Opportunities!

She gestures to the word "OPPORTUNITIES" on the horizon of her drawing. Personal solutions often translate into professional and *vice versa.* A positive change in one area will have a knock-on effect in another. With Eva, there is a further outcome. Her last resolution is:

> 6 See my parents. I'll go to Poland at the end of September. I think I have to accept a simpler relationship with them.

§

Part 5 Six Degrees of Freedom

Chapter 4
In Healing

*Go to your bosom; knock there, and ask your heart
what it doth know.*   Shakespeare, 'Measure for Measure'

MONIKA: I want my back pain to soothe

Monika is the management consultant who injured her back while climbing in the Bavarian Alps. In Part One, I wrote about the start and end of her six rounds of questioning. Here is what happened in between. The section headings are Monika's own, composed immediately after the event while she was writing up the notes she had made during the session with David. I have omitted most of his questions in favor of concentrating on her responses, which are in the condensed form in which she wrote at the time: handy for reading here, because we can get a sense of both the content and the structure of her process at the same time.

David's choice of the Power of Six pattern to use in each round of the salon in Paris was dictated less by the individuality of the client than by the need to work with a group of six people while giving each of them a taste of the three main heuristics: questioning the client at A, the problem at B, and the space between of C (though not, as it turned out, in that order).

After a Clean Start, Monika finds herself seated at a table with her statement, "I want my back pain to soothe and to get back my mobility," in front of her.

MONIKA round 1 ('soothing my pain')
What the problem at B knows

> *And what else could go on there?*   *[repeated]*
> Moving on from something painful, that belongs
> in the past.   [#1 proclaim]
> Connecting with everything in my body.   [#2 explain]
> I want to discover new things.   [#3 reinforce]
> Will untapped resources and talents be revealed?
>   [#4 the wobble]
> I need to feel complete.   [#5 crash & burn]
> To be authentic.   [#6 out of the ashes]
>
> *And* now *what do you know?*
> To find myself I need to let go of the pain from the past.
>   [learning #1]

A hint to herself that the pain may not only be physical.

At the start of each new round, participants are invited to move to another space, or to stay put, or to find a new position. Monika remains at the table for Round Two, but shifted so that she can see the sky outside. Later she reports a feeling while seeking this space of "wanting to be elsewhere."

MONIKA round 2 ('strengthening myself')
What the space of C knows

> *What does that space between you and the statement know?*
>   *[repeated]*
> Connecting with each part of my body and self.
>   [#1 proclaim]
> Starting to like each part.   [#2 explain]
> Feeling happy with each part.   [#3 reinforce]
> It means having to make new movements.   [#4 the wobble]
> It doesn't have the new forces I need.   [#5 crash & burn]
> I have to become a different me and find my equilibrium.
>   [#6 out of the ashes]
> *And* now *what do you know?*
> I become stronger by doing new things. As a result,
> I will change.   [learning #2]

In response to the next invitation to seek another space, Monika lies on the floor.

MONIKA round 3 ('staying connected')
What the client at A knows

> *What do you know there?*   *[repeated]*
> I am learning to breathe.   [#1 proclaim]
> I am learning to listen to my body.   [#2 explain]
> I can be nice and spoil myself.   [#3 reinforce]
> In case of discomfort, I can change myself. [#4 the wobble]
> It means having to really see myself.   [#5 crash & burn]
> So that I can enjoy myself.   [#6 out of the ashes]
>
> *And now what do you know?*
> I have to start by enjoying the NOW.   [learning #3]

For the next round, Monika sits up where she is on the floor. "In expectation," she says later.

MONIKA round 4 ('being myself and using space')
What the client at A knows

We can assume that the "space" in Monika's title refers not only to her physical positioning, but also to the internal spaces she is finding. One parallels the greater freedoms the other is discovering.

> *And what do you know there?*   *[repeated]*
> Feeling.   [#1 proclaim]
> Laughing.   [#2 explain]
> Trying out.   [#3 reinforce]
> Risking.   [#4 the wobble]
> Occasional discomfort.   [#5 crash and burn]
> Enriching.   [#6 out of the ashes]
>
> *And now what do you know?*
> I need to learn new things.   [learning #4]

MONIKA round 5 ('choosing what to do next')
What the client at A knows

Monika gets up from the floor, lounges in an armchair, and puts her feet up on another chair. I learn later that this is something she would never have done in the past because of the pain in her back.

As the session progresses and Monika tries out new things, I notice that her 'wobbles' are taking on the quality of surprise rather than uncertainty, and her 'crashes' the idea of risk rather than failure.

And what do you know there?	*[repeated]*
Taking time.	[#1 proclaim]
Letting things come.	[#2 explain]
Trusting in the process.	[#3 reinforce]
Being curious.	[#4 the wobble]
Needing to talk with others.	[#5 crash & burn]
Wondering.	[#6 out of the ashes]

And now *what do you know?*
If I stay confident and patient then things will happen.
[learning #5]

MONIKA round 6 ('enjoying every moment')
What the client at A knows

This time she stays in the same place and position: in an armchair with her feet up on another chair.

And what do you know there?	*[repeated]*
Using all my senses.	[#1 proclaim]
Being creative.	[#2 explain]
Being beautiful.	[#3 reinforce]
Surprising myself.	[#4 the wobble]
Daring.	[#5 crash & burn]
Taking in.	[#6 out of the ashes]

And now *what do you know?*
The importance of looking around and letting it resonate inside. Everything around me teaches me to enjoy myself in the now. [learning #6 / healing]

Participants are asked to write down six *more* things that they know now. Monika's list is:

1 I can trust myself to find what I need.
2 All will come from looking around
  and listening to the echo inside.
3 I will find enjoyment.
4 New things ahead.
5 I feel optimism.
6 Let's go!

I ask her about the difference between her first statement of the day ("I want my back pain to soothe and to get back my mobility") and her last ("Let's go!"). She says:

> The pain is not the focus any longer. It is in the past. My focus is on now and enjoyment. My place is here, now, with the last statement. All other statements were part of the journey.   [difference]

Her smile takes in the whole group.

MONIKA's Action Plan ('exercising the senses')

A few months after the salon, Monika brings me up to date with the plan she made at the time. In the note below, she describes her original plan, then adds in brackets what actually happened.

> 1 After this session, I will go alone to the park and smell the flowers. (I did this. It helped me process the day.)
>
> 2 Tomorrow, before my first meeting, I shall sit in a café and observe people. (I did this and found it energizing.)
>
> 3 During next week's seminar in Istanbul I will go for a walk alone to smell, listen to, and discover new parts of the town. (I didn't do this, as the hotel was too far out of town, but I had a massage in the hotel instead and took care of myself with gymnastics.)
>
> 4 Before leaving for Istanbul, I will book two tickets for the theatre for my husband and myself for next weekend. (I did this. It did us good to get out of the house together.)
>
> 5 Next weekend I'll go to the park with my children and husband. (Instead, we managed to get away to the coast.

> We now make a point of spending at least part of Sunday together in a park.)

> 6 I will buy myself a bunch of flowers tonight on my way home. (I did this. It was great.)

Nine months after the salon, Monika reports that she is feeling more centered and is able to express her convictions with a great deal more confidence. She has started painting and held her first public exhibition, something she never dreamt of having the courage to do. There had always been an inner voice saying, "You are not good enough ... you can't do this ... you should have known ..."

> I learned to control my inner critic, this well-developed inner voice that had taken over a lot of beliefs from my father. I decided to send the inner critic on a vacation to Hawaii with a one-way ticket! And now I am simply taking things as they come. It is a wonderful feeling.

Healing, as ever, is repair from within.

ERIC: I don't want anythin'!

This is a rather different case of self-healing that took place during a single extended session. It is an example of Grove's trust in the process in spite of every indication that he is doomed to failure.

A therapist colleague who read a draft of this transcript expressed doubts about including the case on the grounds that she would not want inexperienced readers using the Power of Six, or, indeed, any therapeutic procedure, with clients like Eric. I decided to include it as an illustration of Grove at his intuitive, innovative best, but the warning for novice facilitators is clear: take care.

The practice doctor escorts a hugely obese man down the corridor to one of the consulting rooms. ERIC is massively overweight and walks with some difficulty. I guess he is in his thirties, but he looks considerably older. His first words, spoken in a high-pitched, wheezing voice, are:

I don't know why I'm here. The doctor told me to come.

David asks:

So what do you want?

Eric snaps back:

I don't want anythin'!

The doctor reminds Eric of his recurrent nightmare.

Well, I can't sleep. I have this picture.

Where?
In my head. I don't wanna talk about it. Somethin'
happened in the shearin' shed and things have never been
the same since.

What we call in the trade a defining moment, a time in life after
which nothing is ever the same. Despite Eric's reluctance to talk,
this defining moment could hardly have been better expressed.

I can't talk about it. I'm startin' to hurt already. (He weeps)
Well you could write about it or draw it out.

Eric struggles to his feet.

I'm goin' home.

*You can go home. Or you can sit down and draw it out. We
don't have to see it. We're going out for a bit. You can fold
it up or sit on it.*

We leave the room. After a few minutes waiting in the corridor,
we return. Eric is looking distressed. On the table beside him is a
folded piece of paper.

ERIC: a Clean Start

Where does that need to be in the room?
Nowhere.

Put it where it needs to be in relation to you.
No.

\

We're going out of the room again. If you move it, we're gonna know it's moved.

We leave, look at each other, say nothing. After a few minutes, we return. It hasn't moved.

I don't wanna do this. Please can I go?

Eric starts to weep again.

I'm gonna go crazy!

Where does that need to be in relation to you?
I'm gonna break things!

For the first time in our work together, I wonder if David has gone too far. Again, we leave Eric alone. Out in the corridor, I listen in vain for the sound of things breaking. When we return, the paper has been moved a few inches. It has also been turned around. Eric is strangely quiet.

ERIC round 1
What the client at A knows

What do you know about that?		
Well, it seems just a bit lighter.		[#1 proclaim]
And what else do you know?		
The same.		[#2 explain]
And what else do you know?		
Nothin' more.		[#3 reinforce]
And what else do you know?		
I dunno.		[#4 the wobble]
And what else do you know?		
It's still there. I'm goin'.		[#5 crash & burn]

Eric sniffles a bit, but stays where he is. David:

That's only number five. It's the numbers' fault. If it were just up to me, but it's the numbers. What else do you know?

(A pause. Quietly) I dunno. It seems a lot lighter. Maybe
it's lifted.   [#6 out of the ashes]

Clients often surprise me with their about-turn responses in the
sixth iteration, but this is one I never thought possible. When
David and I debrief the session later, he admits to similar doubts,
though not quite as much surprise. A final question to Eric:

And now *what do you know?*

Eric looks at the folded paper on the table and frowns.

I can't see it. I can't see the picture. I can't get it back.
I'm closin' my eyes, but I can't ...   [learning / healing]

We wait. Eric looks at us, checks his watch. For a minute or two,
there is silence. Then a gentle knock at the door. The doctor puts
her head round to report that Eric's transport has arrived. David
tells her:

*Okay, here's what happened. At number five, things got
burned up and at six, something new happened.* (To Eric)
*What's the difference now? I want you to be absolutely
sure it can't come back.*

Eric looks at his little piece of folded paper.

It's nothin'. It really is nothin'.   [difference / healing]

He lifts himself to his feet and makes his way slowly to the door.
Is it my imagination, or is he moving a little more freely? David
comments:

Well, that's what you wanted.

Remarkably (or not, if you knew David), he has remembered what
Eric said at the start: "I don't want anythin'." And that, in an
unusual turnaround – a literal turnaround, if you consider what he
did with his piece of paper – is what he got. "It's nothin'." Spatial
sorting can work in subtle and mysterious ways.

   As we shall see with a very different kind of client.

§

Part Five Six Degrees of Freedom

Chapter 5
In Problem Solving

Perplexity is the beginning of knowledge.   Kahlil Gibran

SILVIE: I need more clients

Silvie is an experienced coach and trainer from Sweden who has been domiciled in France for many years. She has asked me to take her through a Power of Six process with the aim of resolving a situation that has been troubling her for some time.

> Right now, I'm seeing private clients and running workshops at home. It's nice because I like my environment, but I'd like a bigger space for life coaching and corporate work. That requires money I don't have. The way to have more money is to have more corporate clients, but I can't get them until I have the money for a bigger space.

Silvie has articulated a desired outcome (a bigger space), a problem (not enough money for a bigger space), and a solution (more corporate clients to raise the money for a bigger space in which to have more corporate clients), all at the same time. There is a place for this basketful of concerns under problem solving, but there are implications for personal and business development too. It is not an unusual problem and may well derive from deeper issues of identity.

Silvie's approach to resolving or alleviating the particular problem she has constructed at this time in her life derives from her uniqueness. Unique does not mean unusual or rare. There are no shades to being unique, nothing that can be modified by 'almost' or 'very'. The 100 trillion instructions per second of processing that go on in Silvie's brain are quite different to the 100 trillion or so in my brain or yours. A perceived problem, whether it be what to have for supper or what to do with one's life, is specific to the individual, and only the individual and their unconscious will know exactly *how* it is a problem. This is where a self-organizing methodology like the Power of Six comes into its own, because it does not depend on a facilitator's ability to come up with an exemplary solution for every uniquely constructed problem.

Silvie frowns as she replays what she has just said:

> To have more money to get a bigger space I have to have more corporate clients and I can't get more corporate clients until I have a bigger space, which means finding more money. That's a real double bind, isn't it?

The procedures of the Power of Six could have been made for exploring and resolving double binds, dilemmas, and the rest.

> *Double bind* two irreconcilable demands
> *Dilemma* two equally satisfactory or unsatisfactory alternatives
> *False syllogism* two equally valid statements producing an invalid conclusion ("Mavis feels sad; I once felt sad; I know how Mavis is feeling")

Systems thinker Gregory Bateson analyzed what was going on in these 'dissonant cognitions'. The person is receiving contrary emotional injunctions, and there is no point in an outsider asking which of the messages is more valid or dismissing them both as nonsensical. And yet for their failure to fulfill the conflicting injunctions, the victims will often punish themselves – in Silvie's case, through anxiety, inertia, and a sense of failure.

I could say to myself that I 'understand' Silvie's problem, but I really don't. Fortunately for Silvie, my options as an Emergent Knowledge facilitator in response to her rhetorical "That's a real double bind, isn't it?" are limited pretty much to "What do you know about that?" and the one I choose:

Find a space that knows about that.

I suggest this because Silvie is restless. She is prowling around the room while talking. Her higher nervous system is making projections of the right mental space to be in, while her body is using the room as a physical metaphor for the search.

SILVIE: a Clean Start

Silvie explores the house where we are working and eventually decides that the space with the information she needs is in the kitchen. How we find the spaces that know what we need to know has an element of mystery, but it happens. We know when a space feels right. The positioning of our bodies in relation to both the physical and intangible elements that define the space will often be very specific, arrived at by a process of trial and error and increasingly fine adjustments.

Silvie finds herself at the kitchen table, seated at an angle that gives her a view outside to the garden. "I don't know why I chose this space," she says, "it just feels right." I invite her to:

> *Choose the size of paper you want and write or draw what*
> *it is you want to work on.*

She sketches out a diagram in two parts, 'X' and 'Y' (Figure 37).

Figure 37. Silvie's choice

She explains:

> X is the problem – needing more money – and Y is the
> solution – getting more business. The trouble is I can't get X
> if I don't have Y. So I'm stuck and I don't know what to do.

Mapping out the problem in this way (she has already decided to
omit the third, complicatory, element of wanting a bigger space) is
helping Silvie simplify and clarify the bind. Her stuckness is now
explicit.

The problem – needing more money to generate more business
– is in a state of spatial and visual equilibrium with the solution –
generating more business to make more money. As usual in this
kind of stand-off, neither side is willing to make the first move.

My next invitation is:

> *Place that* [the paper] *where it needs to be and place
> yourself where you are now in relation to it.*

I guide Silvie through a standard Clean Start to establish her
structural relationship to the problem at B in position, direction,
angle, and height. She remains at the table throughout and
discovers that the double bind she wants to work on is made up,
not surprisingly, of *two* Bs. To represent this, she takes a pair of
kitchen scissors and cuts her statement in two.

One piece, the supposed problem, 'X' (needing more money),
remains nearby on the table in the space of B_1. The other, the
apparent solution, 'Y' (generating more business), requires a move
into the future, and after some exploration is pinned to a tree in the
garden in the space of B_2.

Silvie returns to the kitchen table. She has symbolized her
relationship to the bind by creating two spaces: the space of C_1
between her and the problem on the table; and the space of C_2
between her and the 'solution' outside. Just as she is about to
confirm this arrangement, she realizes:

> Ah. The problem is not in the right place. It needs to be lower.

She moves the B_1 problem onto a shelf under the table and places
her hand on the tabletop above (Figure 38).

Figure 38. Silvie's double bind

> This is very much how it is. The problem doesn't go away,
> but there are always things on top – the family, the need for
> lunch, dinner – to keep in touch with, literally. The table is
> important.

As the client has adjusted the relative positions of A and B_1, I need
to ask her the Clean Start questions again. When I ask if the
problem at B_1 is at the right angle, something changes for Silvie.
She reaches below the table and turns the paper round to face the
other way.

> Ah, I have turned my problem around! I thought the
> problem was needing more money, but actually it's
> needing more corporate clients.

Another 'turnaround', reminiscent of Eric's. Silvie's is an interim,
rather than a concluding, move, but it marks an important change.
At the start, "I need more money" was inextricably mixed with "I
need more corporate clients," two different desires that somehow
combined into the bind of thinking that the only way to have one
was to have the other. Now Silvie has found a way of adjusting
their relative importance. The bind may already be loosening.

The Clean Start procedure *itself* is helping Silvie to deconstruct the problem. Note the importance of asking all the Clean Start questions. If I had omitted "Is that at the right angle?" the turnaround of the paper at B_1 might not have happened. The fact that Silvie had represented the problem on paper made it easier for her to move it. And finding a physical equivalent to the mental adjustment helped her confirm and further the mental shift.

The unusual demands of a Clean Start have also activated the creativity that Silvie will need to resolve the problem. In spite of the formulaic detachment of the Power of Six protocol, this is not a passive experience. It requires the client's active emotional, physical, and imaginative engagement.

SILVIE round 1
What the client at A knows

I nod towards the statement under the table at B_1 and the statement in the garden at B_2.

> *What do you know about those?*

Using "those" rather than "that" keeps the two-ness of the bind in the client's awareness. It is not my job to resolve the bind. If the procedure had a purpose at this point, it would be to focus Silvie's attention on the problem and not to diminish it in any way.

My next few questions are omitted so that you can follow the ebb and flow of Silvie's process more easily:

> I can see what I want on the tree. My problem is out of sight under the table, but my hand is reminding me it's still there. There's tension between the three of us – me, the problem, what I want – and a kind of stability, unfortunately. (Pauses)

> I have a pain in my right shoulder. This is how it is. I'm keeping an eye on my outcome and a hand on my problem, and the pain is reminding me how I am struggling.

> [#1, 2, 3, 4; proclaim, explain, reinforce, the wobble]

And what else do you know?
There are two Swedish words – *ta itu.* Do it now. Just do what needs to be done. But this position stops me. I can't.

[#5 crash and burn]

And what else do you know?
I clearly don't want to have the pain in my shoulder, but there's something about moving my hand related to what's under the table ... I would like to hit it! (She hits the table very hard) If I really *do* it, I need to have lots of energy to break through in order to attend to what's under.

[#6 out of the ashes]

And now *what do you know?*
I realize I have two ways of dealing with the problem: keep my hand on the table and the tension in my shoulder, or really deal with it – break what is between the problem and me. But I need to find a different way which is not a breaking the table kind of way!

[learning #1]

SILVIE round 2
What the problem at B₁ knows

Silvie shakes off her fixed position and retrieves the paper at B₁ from under the table. She uses the kitchen scissors to cut the paper into pieces, and as she does so explains:

Each piece contains a little part of the problem.

It has become second nature to me to count the number of times clients do certain things. Silvie's first and second cuts produce three strips of paper ... each of which she cuts in two ...

Figure 39. Five cuts = six pieces

In doing so (Figure 39), she produces – without the least prompting from anything but the system – six pieces. She spreads these out on the table and moves them around, deliberately at first, like pieces on a chessboard, and then more spontaneously. She is creating a fluid, intuitive information network. Each piece adds its intelligence to the others like honey bees communing in their search for a new hive. Eventually, a new direction for the swarm emerges:

> This is like some kind of opening. There is something evident to be done, but it has no words. I am in another space.   [learning #2]

SILVIE round 3
What the problem or the space knows

I nod towards the papers that hold Silvie's original statement. I have no idea if they still represent the original problem at B_1 or have morphed into new information in the spaces of C and D.

> *What do they know?*

Silvie re-sorts them silently. I suppose her to be making a statement of some kind to herself.   *[#1 proclaim]*

> *And what else do they know?*

She writes on one of the pieces of paper, then continues writing on the remaining pieces of paper.   *[#2 explain]*

> *And what else do they know?*
> They represent different things required to achieve my outcome.   [#3 reinforce]

> *And what else do they know?*
> So many things to do. (She pauses) Too many.
>   [#4 the wobble]

> *And what else do they know?*
> It feels overwhelming.   [#5 crash and burn]

> *And what else do they know?*
> Oh.

A pause. When Silvie speaks again, her voice has a different quality:

> Something has shifted. My outcome [at B_2 in the garden] is nearer. It's coming in from the cold and it's not so far in front of me. The space that was two years away is now more like six to nine months.   [#6 out of the ashes]

> *And* now *what do they know?*

She picks out two of the pieces.

> These two have priority. They're realistic. They're actually possible. One is to have corporate clients and workshops, individuals or groups, in a rented space. The other is to have private clients, individuals, who can be in a rented space or a home space. If they want to work with me, they'll work with me wherever I am.   [learning #3]

> *And now what do* you *know?*
> These are the answers to the initial money problem. Meanwhile, I can keep my global outcome and see it right in front of me rather than out there in the garden. I still get a sense of broad support from the ground outside, but also I get it from my own hands here.   [learning #3]

SILVIE rounds 4, 5, and 6
Client self-learning

When a self-motivated client is well into their own process, the multiple six can take on a more concentrated form, as happens here. There is a parallel with what tree ecologists call 'telescoping'. A stage of growth that is apparently missing will actually be present but hidden, like one of the tubes of a telescope that has not been fully extended. Silvie continues to process silently. I wait. At a certain point, I ask again:

> *And what else do you know now?*
> I don't have to worry. And I don't have to hurt myself by breaking the table! (She smiles for the first time) At the same time, I can keep the quality of looking out there.

She looks out of the window to the garden where her original outcome used to be.

> And that's very important. I can keep the quality of being sunny in here even when it's raining there. (She laughs) It's an ability to *ta itu* – to just do what has to be done, without having to break the home environment.
>
> [learning #4]

Silvie seems to have taken herself through a fourth round. She is sitting more comfortably now.

> *And what else do you know now?*
> The tension in my shoulder has gone. I'm breathing differently. (She places both hands on the table) I'm keeping my connection to the problem while looking ahead. And my hands can move. I have mobility.
>
> [learning #5]

> *And what else do you know now?*
> There's a time for taking care of one thing and a time for taking care of the other, and there's a great benefit in restricting or focusing on one specific area rather than trying to solve everything at the same time.
>
> [learning #6]

Silvie decides that this is as far as she needs to go for the moment. Rather than being taken through three facilitator-led rounds, she has come up with three self-generated learnings. Enough to keep her occupied for a while.

SILVIE's Action Plan

Silvie lists five behaviors related to finding a rented space, clearing her home space, and doing her accounts and administration.

> *And a sixth?*
> Mm, I'm going to take a day off in the country.

Ah, the optional extra that takes on compelling importance. If I had not seen her plan pedantically through to a sixth item and

Silvie had settled for purely work-related behaviors, she may never have got around to the one thing that may well energize the rest.

Some weeks later, Silvie tells me that she chose to sit at the kitchen table because it is the hub of the house, a domestic metaphor that related to her eventual solution, which was about making creative use of what was already available.

> My action plan was easy to write. It had different levels in it. The actions were realistic and achievable, and directly related to my two original pieces of paper. They solve the immediate problem *and* they contribute to the global outcome. I keep the image of my global outcome, the two pieces of paper, and my action plan as reminders. Going back to them reactivates the dynamism and ease I experienced during the process.

I wonder how the outcome will affect Silvie's deeper sense of herself. Eight months after the session when she reads this account, she tells me that she doesn't understand how she could have been so blind to the obvious at the time:

> There really never was a problem!

Sometimes the obvious only stares us in the face when we take the time to reflect on it. Now, says Silvie:

> I'm running the workshops at home and the space is big enough to accommodate the number of people I like to have at those workshops. It's fine when I work with individuals too – the environment is actually nice for them. Working from home gives me a lot of flexibility. And when I work with companies, the need for a bigger space is taken care of because the space is rented as part of the budget for the workshop.

The problem, it turns out, was neither the money nor the clients, but how to make the best use of existing resources. And by my reckoning, the most important resource was Silvie herself.

§

Part Five Six Degrees of Freedom

Chapter 6
In Business Development

Ipsa Scientia Potestas Est. For also knowledge itself is power.
Francis Bacon

JULIA: problems and possibilities
What the client at A knows

Julia is a Paris-based consultant, experienced, positive, curious, and a little bit wary. She is considering going into business with an American colleague who wants to open an office in France.

> I want to explore the problems and possibilities of working with him.

Julia tells me that her colleague is a highly regarded individual, but he can be difficult and demanding, so she needs to plan carefully. After a thorough Clean Start, she sits facing her written outcome, which she has placed on a nearby chair as though she were in conversation with the man himself. Gestalt therapists would appreciate the two-chair set-up. NLP practitioners might see an opportunity for an exercise in 'perceptual positions'. But here is an alternative that does not involve the client swapping chairs back and forth at the behest of the therapist.

> *What do you know about that* [the statement on the chair at B] *from there* [where Julia is at A]?
> I know a comfortable distance. I want to keep the right distance.   [#1 proclaim]

It would have been difficult, if not impossible, for Julia to access the information held at the right distance if I had invited her to move to the perceptual position of her colleague. This would have been more in pursuit of another agenda ('to get Julia to see the situation from her colleague's point of view,' perhaps), rather than the client's own, which she has expressed very clearly as "to keep the right distance." In any case, I am bound by two key constraints: I must honor the A → C → B construct that Julia has built inch by inch during her Clean Start procedure; and I must stick to the same heuristic with which I began.

> *And what else do you know from there?*
> I know it would be good for me to be clear about healthy boundaries – to separate out the issues before committing.
>   [#2 explain]

> *And what else do you know from there?*
> If I give that priority and get clarity, that is enough healthy boundaries.   [#3 reinforce]

> *And what else do you know from there?*
> Well, I don't want this to be mixed up with everything else.
>   [#4 the wobble]

In most other modalities, I would have wanted to know more about that "everything else". Here I can accept that the client herself knows well enough. It is an item of information that will iterate with every other item that came before and will follow. It does not have to be explained to me or deconstructed to play its part in Julia's immediate process.

> *And what else do you know from there?*
> I fear the boundaries are not respected. This could be a real mismatch.   [#5 crash and burn]

> *And what else do you know from there?*
> If the boundaries are respected, the idea is a good one.
>   [#6 out of the ashes]

> *And now what do you know?*
> I get a lovely image of one of the Tarot cards, *L'Imperatrice* ['The Empress']. She sits with a scepter held in her right hand and a shield in her left hand. She is seated on what she knows. I've been used to being the Priestess

hiding behind a veil. She is my past. *L'Imperatrice* sits, she
is my inspiration, and when I sit like this, she is my
guarantee, my guide.   [learning]

Julia sits back, smiles, rocks back and forth in her chair.

She has weight. She does not flit. She feels very French to
me. Very individual.

She nods to herself, murmurs:

Hm. Hm. Hm.
And what do those three hms know?

A question on loan from Clean Language. It aims to help Julia
articulate the information she has embodied in these three
meaningful murmurs. She reaches deep for the response:

Ah. The first knows that *L'Imperatrice* comes from way
down. Timeless and soundless.

The second?
Ah, yes. It is the same place as the shield, protecting the
heart. The third goes up to the eyes in recognition. Yes, I
can see that.

And now what do you know?

The learning question brings Julia back to herself.

I know that if I listen to my voice and find the resonating
places in my body, I become intelligent. I know that giving
respect to the first is giving form to the second. The first is
the place where I know my colleague and his business best.
There is a deep knowing in the sound, the music, the poetry
of it. Not the heady stuff.   [learning]

*Given what you know now, what is the difference between
that and what you knew at the start?*
If I had not done this, I would not have got to the richness
of these possibilities. Even if the guy can be very difficult
for me to deal with, I can see the enormous possibilities.
The difference now is about looking at it head on and
having strategies in place.   [difference]

Not all business development issues will go to places like this, but I suspect that more might succeed if they did. Julia calls her Action Plan 'Boundaries and Opportunities'. Each behavioral point in the plan relates specifically to what she will and will not do, when and where, to develop her relationship with her colleague and his company in ways that respect her personal ethos. The last point on the plan is, as she says:

> Just for me. To look at the *Imperatrice* card when I get home, and consider the hidden world of the sound and the feminine voice.

Figure 40. Julia's new knowing

And what ensued was a negotiation that gave both parties what they wanted. The American colleague gained a European base, and Julia's influence and business expanded. There were other benefits. On more than one occasion, Julia's colleague was heard to say that he had been surprised and gratified by what Julia had brought to the arrangement. "She has got it together," he would say. Julia would not claim that a single Power of Six session was responsible for her getting it together, because she had other resources, but she used the process (as did Monika in *Healing*) to consider, confirm, and continue a path she was already drawn to take. The process helped her to face the issues squarely, and gave her the impetus to put both long and short term strategies in place.

§

In Part Five, we looked at the pivotal role played by the Power of Six in the personal and professional development of:

Sandra	Losing weight
Simon	Sorting my head out
Eva	Being myself
Monika	Healing and moving on
Eric	Wanting nothing
Silvie	Solving the money problem
Julia	Establishing boundaries, creating opportunities.

The basic seeking and finding patterns we saw in practice were:

Making a Clean Start
Questioning the Client at A
Questioning the Problem at B
Questioning the Space Between of C
Compiling an Action Plan.

The sixth and final Part of the book looks at emerging applications of the Power of Six and shares a few ideas for taking the basic techniques further.

Part Six

EMERGING

1 Moves

2 Numbers

3 Witnesses

4 Teams

5 Reflections

6 Prescriptions

Sometimes I've believed as many as six impossible things before breakfast. Lewis Carroll

Part Six Emerging

Introduction

The essence of knowledge is, having it, to apply it. Confucius

David Grove was not one to rest on his considerable achievement of creating six groundbreaking methodologies in Clean Language, Therapeutic Metaphor, Intergenerational Healing, Clean Space, Emergent Knowledge, and The Power of Six. He was possessed by the need to go further, deeper, and cleaner. "I am a chaser of ideas," he would say. This was more the purposeful foraging of a bee than the random flutterings of a butterfly. He had an intuitive idea of where he was going and was forever open to what he would find there.

For strategic (not to say pedantic) reasons, I tried to restrict the ideas and applications here to a certain number. I failed. Emergence could not be contained. Here are eleven applications of the Power of Six in psychotherapy, self-development, and corporate coaching, though I have managed to fit them into six broad categories: 'Moves', 'Numbers', 'Witnesses', 'Teams', 'Reflections' and 'Prescriptions'.

Two themes run through chapters: one towards greater architectural simplicity, the other providing support for more elaborate structures. Half the ideas here originated with Grove, some came up in discussions with him, and some were created as a result of his influence. I have included those we always planned to mention at the end of the book, a few more I think of as having 'legs' for the future, and one or two that are more experimental.

There are others in development. Dr. Vishwamohan Thakur, a consultant psychiatrist in India, is taking the Power of Six into his work with the mentally ill and has begun teaching the techniques in medical school. In France, Jennifer de Gandt and Lynn Bullock are combining the Power of Six with movement and vision therapies, Tania Korsak is exploring applications in child development, Lynne Burney in corporate trainings and Silvie de Clerck in her creativity workshops. In Britain, Carol Wilson and Angela Dunbar are applying the numbers to coaching theory and practice. Maurice Brasher meanwhile is defining the very idea of emergence and Emergent Knowledge as a theoretical foundation for all this work.

The Australian counselor and educator Patrick Lynch is using the Power of Six in teaching, in spirituality retreats, and in his clinical practice, which involves supporting children and adults with terminal illnesses. He writes to me:

> Whenever a client makes some sort of definitive statement such as "I'm no good at relationships" or "I should have done more," I ask permission to do a process with them. I say it is repetitive in nature and therefore may get a little frustrating, but that it is in the repetition (and by extension, the frustration) where the value lies. And then I go through the questions.

Lynch has found that even if clients do not have a focus to begin with, a clear one will emerge from their early answers. The more superficially 'known' material appears first, giving the deeper-seated, more useful information a chance to emerge in the later responses. Thus, he says:

> There is a deepening and unfolding of their process in a simple and elegant manner. The more I use it for my clients and for myself (and I use it all the time about anything that bothers me), *the more confidence I have in it.*

My italics. It is what happened to me and what other facilitators tell me: the more you use it, the more confidence you have in it.

Lynch keeps verbatim notes of his clients' responses and if the next step isn't entirely clear, he invites them to pick out what he calls "the juiciest" bits of what they have said and to repeat the process. This is an interesting variation on the standard model. In the hands of a naïve or overzealous facilitator (the kind I have characterized elsewhere as wanting actively to change things rather than simply to facilitate), a process involving selection would be deemed 'unclean' by EK standards if it involved any kind of value appraisal of the client's information. But if the words of the 'juicy bits' are *strictly the client's own*, and if their selection is *strictly the client's own*, the new input into the system will be clean. And as I said at the start, my intention with this book is not just that you should get to know the formula, but that you should get into the frame of mind of someone who uses it to do new things. No formula was ever the last word on a subject.

If the client has no objection to note taking or recording, it is a habit I recommend. There can be extra benefit from seeing or hearing yourself over, as Corinne found so movingly (in *What the System Knows*), even months after her process.

Some of the applications and exercises here will no doubt appear in a variety of likenesses as the Clean and Emergent communities continue to develop and refine Grove's original work. I ask three things of developers: always credit David Grove as the begetter, further his philosophy of working for the common good, and in his spirit honor the principle of a continuous learning community. If you find yourselves training or facilitating others, do it to the extent that they wish to be trained or facilitated, by code-congruently applying the principles of self-organization: "What is it that you wish to learn/do/work on?" "What do you know about that?" and so on. Emergence is more an attitude of mind than a set of techniques. It cannot, by definition, be frozen in time or form.

Before we go further, a reminder of the fundamental tenets against which all Emergent Self Knowledge developments may be measured:

> we are all unique;
> we create our own problems;
> we resolve them in our own way.

Since individual problems are structured to our unique personalities and perceptions, our uniqueness has to be the source of every solution. To retrieve the information we need in order to 're–cognize' and reorganize, we have to tap the inner worlds of our own wisdom. There are countless therapies and methods devoted to doing this, of course. If there is a difference with the Power of Six, it is that when it works, it practically obliges the client to achieve the changes they need. If a facilitator follows the process faithfully, for some clients at least there is no escape. And remarkably and desirably, they will discover what they need to know for themselves.

For a search and discovery pattern to conform to Power of Six principles it should abide – for the time being at least, for emergence will do its own thing – by the conditions I outlined in Part One:

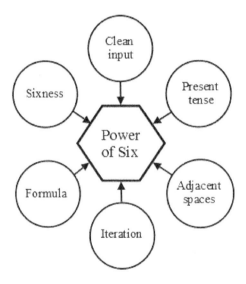

Figure 41. Six necessary conditions for the Power of Six

1 *Clean Input.* Are all questions minimally assumptive, non- suggestive, metaphor-free, and based on what the client knows?

2 *Present Tense.* Is all questioning, information, or knowledge elicited and accessed in the here and now?

3 *Spatiality and Adjacency.* Are all sources of information treated as, or presumed to be, occupying neighboring conceptual / symbolic or physically located nodes or spaces?

4 *Iteration.* Does the information in each response feed back iteratively to enhance the next, leading to a collapse of complexity from which self-reorganized healing or resolution can emerge?

5 *Formula.* Is every part of the process formulaic, teachable, and reproducible, and designed to encourage clients to discover what they need to know for themselves?

6 *Sixness.* Do the key parts of the process depend on, or stem from, the cumulative qualities of a set, network, or series of six?

Bear these criteria in mind as you consider a number of ideas and exercises. Allow yourself to be the still center around which these new worlds turn.

§

Part Six Emerging

Chapter 1

Moves: A Turn in Space
        The Six-Space Symptom

I may not have gone where I intended to go, but I have ended up where I needed to be.   Douglas Adams

A Turn In Space

Figure 42. A device for taking pedestrians off their predictable paths:
Anna on the gyroscope with David facilitating
and accomplice Maurice in attendance

'Psychogeography' is the study of the relationship between spaces and people. Grove worked in the expectation that when the bodymind's relationship with space changes, so do our ways of thinking and feeling. He was adept at taking pedestrians off their predictable paths (Figure 42).

"I was strapped in," ANNA reports a couple of months after her experience on the gyroscope, "but felt as free as a bird. It gave me the mental and emotional freedom to go anywhere I wanted. I rediscovered the abilities I needed to achieve my goals. The only person stopping me was myself."

Anna is a thoughtful, purposeful woman. At the age of six, she made a conscious decision to realize her parents' dream, which had been to leave Warsaw one day to live in a country at peace. She moved to France in her early twenties to work for Amnesty International, studied NLP, and trained in Clean Language and Symbolic Modeling. I first meet Anna at a seminar in Normandy centered on students' personal projects. Hers is "To teach Clean Language and 'La Modélisation Symbolique' in the Rhône-Alpes, Paris, and Poland; but my project is so vague and vast," she complains, "it has no boundaries; it is more like a dream."

David guides Anna through a series of Clean and Power of Six processes to develop her project and then invites her to take a turn on the gyroscope, a device made up of three rotating rings, each of which can be spun on its own axis to allow freedom of movement in any direction. The gyroscope is mounted on a trailer and parked in the grounds of the training facility. Anna sits at the center of the rig, securely strapped to the seat and suspended in space. David asks her:

> *What do you know here and now?*
> I see trees. The trees hide the forest beyond. There is information I cannot see in the fields between them. Somehow, I have to have this information in order to realize my project.

A typical A→C→B set-up: Anna on the gyro is at A, her problem ("to realize my project") somewhere in the distant forest at B, and what she needs ("information") in the fields of C between them. There is slight complication to the problem represented by the trees in the foreground, which obscure both the forest and the fields.

David and his stand-in assistant Maurice turn the drive wheel of the gyroscope until Anna tells them to stop. She is tilted at 30 degrees to the vertical.

And what do you know there?
Good. I can see the track beyond the trees.

The complicatory element in her 'reality metaphor' has already cleared and new information, "the track beyond," has appeared. This may be Anna's metaphor for 'the way ahead.'

It has posts at regular intervals. They remind me of my project.

Another turn on the gyroscope until the client says:

That's it. Stop there. (She is about 45 degrees to the vertical)

And what do you know there
The repeating posts on the road are like a reference for my project, which is to relay what I know for others to pass on. (Another turn) Stop there.

And what do you know there?
It's strange. I have a center of gravity that can move.

True enough. She is almost upside-down. It is a surreal scene, but the interesting thing for me as observer is not that Anna has a center of gravity that can move, but that she has chosen the fourth iteration in which to feel "strange" (Figure 43).

Figure 43. David follows Anna's instructions

You will know the six-step process well enough by now, so I shall not record every question or categorize every response. The only thing you need to know that makes this exercise different to the others is that before every question the client is turned in space until they indicate a place to stop, at which precise point the apparatus is secured and the facilitator asks, "What do you know there?" The client responds and the gyroscope is turned again. After six such turns, the facilitator asks the learning question, "And now what do you know?" There might then be another round of six, perhaps another, until the client is ready to stop.

I have chosen Anna's process to illustrate the gyroscopic journey, not because of what she can see in reality – trees, fields, and so on (after all, clients may choose to report on their inner visions) – but because the increasing awareness of herself and her project that Anna describes neatly parallels her multi-dimensional experience *and* its metaphorical equivalent.

You will get the idea as we travel with Anna on this orbit around herself. Here is a potted version of her words, translated from the French, but sans questions, sans analysis. You could test your knowledge of the numbers by mapping a notional hexad onto her narrative, or you could simply note what repetition and iteration generate: new, highly relevant, information and eventual emergence. As in all good metaphors, the literal and symbolic are at times indistinguishable:

> I can move like a very slow pendulum, back and forth over my project ... Ah, it is a *linking* movement. That's it. A movement back and forth that *relays information* ...

> Hm. There is something about having a fixed point of view, but also being able to move freely and flexibly. Continue ...

> Good, I see a tree. The tree has information for me. It has roots. And it is solid. It is solid because it has roots. And it also has a direction of growth and multiple branches. There are many trees, each one individual.

> But what do I need for my project? I have lost sight of it. My head feels as if it is on back to front. At the same time, the world is more beautiful. It's as if I could fly. I can fly over my project with a larger vision. Go on ...

234 The Power of Six

That's new and uncomfortable, but gives me an interesting perspective. I see the earth, the sky, the trees, but when everything moves, it is impossible to find a point of reference. I need to know where I am in order to report it. Continue ...

Stop. No, go back a bit. There.

I am always fascinated by how precisely clients know where to stop. A fraction of a degree can make all the difference. This is somatic, not cognitive, knowing. The client finds a place where the sensory and motor maps of the bodymind are functioning without interference. It is as if the space has chosen the client rather than the other way round. Anna recognizes that something feels different or significant *just here, right now.*

This is a good position. Something appears. It is telling me something about the back and forth, the relaying between myself and others, and our ways of seeing and feeling. That's beautiful ...

But there is also danger. If I go only in the direction of beauty, I lose sight of my project. I fall into my old contemplative ways. I could stay a long time there and that's not good for my project. Go further ...

There. I am stable again. I see everything as if I had circular vision. There. Thank you.

It is equally typical of the process that clients know when they have gone far enough, which considerably reduces the need for facilitator guesswork. Clients learn to negotiate their own process. They become agents for themselves.

And now *what do you know?*
I see where I am. I have beauty and contemplation in a space where I can take care of myself. But there need to be limits, boundaries to that. On the gyroscope, my whole body can move, and now there is a synergy between external and internal movement. It's not one or the other, but both. And it is learning how to be free. I used to have a

concept of liberty as a field, an empty space. And now it's ... it's like the freedom of an infant.

Anna frowns. Her face sets for a moment. Then:

> But there is something else, something missing. There is a lack of liberty, a lack of space, of money, of love, that push me on.

> *And what else do you know?*
> I learn that in this lack there is also freedom. I am not obliged any more to escape. And I have more information about 'relaying'. The motivation comes from me and if I am working with the right people, the information is passed on.

A month later, Anna returns for a second session. She reports that the first turn in space served to make her project "visible" to her.

> My goal now is to assume a leadership role. To get in touch with my identity as a leader and my ability to get a project team together to make things happen.

At the end of the session, she reports not only having a clearer vision of her project, but also a physical feel for it. It has become embodied. Meaning and ownership have merged as a result of engaging emotionally, conceptually, and kinesthetically with her metaphor.

Anna goes on to integrate her teaching project with her mission in life, which she identifies as "To bring peace to people," a calling that stems from the history of her family during the second world war, through the Warsaw uprising of 1944 and the post-war Soviet occupation. A few months after this session, she reports:

> The work I did on the gyroscope helped me link all these things. I have since improved my visibility, produced brochures, presented at two conferences, co-created a website and set up a training institute in Warsaw.

Her project has also seen a significant refinement. It is now:

> To train Symbolic Modeling and Emergent Knowledge in
> Poland for the next ten years.

There are a number of embryonic variations on the gyroscope – tilt boards, rigs on wheels, and giant balls (see the 'Zorb Ball' and the 'Virtusphere' in the References) – that come into the category of 'A Turn in Space.' What they all have in common is the capacity for offering the client many more psychoactive positions than are available at ground level. Such devices can be happily adapted for the purpose of (somewhat unorthodox) psychotherapy and self-development, but given their size, cost, and the need for two attendants to operate safely, it may be a while before they catch on in the average consulting room.

The next logical progression will be to facilitate clients while weightless in space, or in a wind tunnel, or while skydiving. In all of these, very small movements make a big difference, I am told. Do let me know how you get on.

The Six-Space Symptom

A few months before he died, Grove told me that he thought this next process was "such an amazing discovery, so amazingly, blindingly obvious, yet we missed it all these years." The exercise combines elements of Clean Language, Clean Space, Therapeutic Metaphor, and the Power of Six in a seamless procedure aimed at relieving or resolving a physical or psychological symptom. Assuming that the client has already introduced or articulated such a symptom, the process starts by simply inviting the client to:

> *Find a space to be in.*

Once in place, the client is facilitated to generate a 'feeling' image or metaphor for the symptom with the standard Clean Language question:

> *And that is an X* [the symptom exactly as described by the client] *like what?*

The answer might be "knot in my stomach," "heavy heart," "weight on my shoulders" and so on. The metaphor is developed with standard Clean questioning ("And does X have a size or shape?" "And what kind of X?" etc.). The client is particularly encouraged to find out more about the *location* of the metaphor in their sense of bodymind space ("And where is ...?" "And whereabouts is ...?"). They are then invited to:

Move to another space.

In which the facilitator, in the knowledge that the client already has the experience of *something there* in terms of either the symptom or the space or both, introduces an ambiguous:

And what is there now?

"There" could refer to the space or the metaphor or a combination of both. The response is likely to indicate that the metaphor-in-the-space is evolving or modifying in some way.

The facilitator may ask basic Clean questions ("What kind of X?" "Is there anything else about X?" and so on) to help the client clarify what is happening, then:

Move to another space.
And what is there now?

And so on, for six spaces in all. Until finally:

Move to a space that knows about all of that.
And now *what do you know?*

Given the likely evolution of the metaphor as a result of the networking effect of six adjacent spaces, either the client will have more insight into their condition and the option of going on to another round, or the symptom will have self-healed.

JOHN is a semi-retired academic concerned that the twinges of pain he has been experiencing in his right knee presage an age-related disability. I invite him to:

Find a space to be in.

Space #1. He gets up from the easy chair on which he was sitting and moves to an upright chair. I employ the full Clean Language syntax. The first part confirms John's exact words:

> And *twinges of pain in right knee ...*

The second part repeats them, prefaced by 'And when ...' to reorient the client into the explicit here-and-nowness of his symptom:

> and when *twinges of pain in right knee ...*

which sets up the third part, the powerful metaphor-eliciting Clean question:

> *twinges of pain in right knee are* like what?
> Like an amoeba with six or seven rays or threads coming out of it.

Further questioning develops the symbol's attributes and location. I won't repeat the full Clean Language syntax here, because it's a bit of a bore having to read it before every question, but I do stress its importance in the live process in establishing a rich, complete, and present relationship between client, symptom, and metaphor. If you know the syntax already, I encourage you to use all three parts. If you don't, I urge you to learn them (and the rationale behind them).

> *[...] And is there anything else about an amoeba with six or seven rays coming out of it?*
> It's kind of splat shaped and pinkish.

> *[...] And whereabouts in right knee is splat shaped pinkish amoeba?*
> About half an inch in, just there.

John indicates a precise place on the inside of his right knee. I invite him now to:

> *Move to another space.*

Space #2. John gets up and finds a place a meter or two away. I direct my ambiguous time, space, and matter question both to the metaphor *and* to the place he has moved:

> *And what is there now?*
> Well, I'm seeing it kind of projected onto a screen just in front of me, and it's got movement now – a flowing out from the center.

John is projecting his pain into a physical/conceptual space 'outside' himself. He will probably be able to deal with it more effectively there than he can in his knee. After a moment for him to familiarize himself with the image, I invite him to:

> *Move to another space.*

Space #3. John moves to what he describes as "the other side of the projection screen."

> *And what is there now?*
> I'm aware of a cone of light from the projector. Some sort of microscope is projecting an image on the screen from my knee.
>
> (Another slight pause) *Move to another space.*

Space #4. John moves to what he calls "just in front of the projector."

> *And what is there now?*
> There are connections to my knee, a bunch of cables. If I move my knee and jiggle it, the image moves about a bit. That feels uneasy.
>
> *Move to another space.*

Space #5. John decides to lie on his back.

> I'm looking up at the cone of light and the screen from below.

If (privately) I were to interpret the unease John felt at #4 as a 'wobble', I might view his position on the floor now at #5 as a near literal 'crash'!

And what is there now?
There's dust in the beam of light and some kind of thing stuck on my knee. It goes inside like a CT scan. Hm. It reminds me of my terminally ill cousin.

Move to another space.

Space #6. John gets up from the floor. Most clients are likely to have such a well-defined visual or embodied sense of their metaphor landscape by now that they will be able to choose where to move spatially in relation to any part of it. John describes the quality of his visual and kinesthetic metaphor as:

> A bit like a hologram. Three-dimensional, but transparent and clearly illusory. It has a fixed location and I can walk up to it as if it were real. The image of the projector doesn't stop me seeing the room beyond and around it.

Move to a space that knows about all of that.

John now moves to a place he describes as "behind the projector."

> Ah. This is a 'medical' position. I can control what is going on in the knee and do what I have to do to soothe whatever is in the knee. It's strange. It's as if I'm a narrator, as if I had a residual feeling from the past that I'm telling a story about. The image has become a memory, a slide on the projector. It hasn't removed the twinges, but it has made them acceptable. Something that worried me is no longer a cause of concern.

> *And now what do you know?*
> I know I can have a kind of image of the knee and by moving it around I can change things. And I know I can live with it. It's there, but not fixed.

> *And what is the difference between what you knew at the start and what you know now?*
> What's the difference? I have more degrees of freedom. It's easier to move my knee sensibly. And now I have a control screen from which to manage it.

I help John develop his "degrees of freedom" and "control screen" with Clean questioning on the lines of "How many degrees?" "What kind of control?" "And then what happens?" etc.

"There is no question," John tells me some months later, "that the act of creating the projector and then being able to move around it to see it from different locations, successfully opened out my perception of the knee so that I could see more ways of managing it. Having an externalized image helps me to see it in a more rounded way and that gives me more options."

§

Part Six Emerging

Chapter 2
Numbers: Natural Numbers
The Ordinal Six

It is more difficult to be simple than to be complicated. John Ruskin

My mission here is to make it easier to be simple. Not everything reduces to a formula, but a formulaic procedure can cut through unnecessary complications.

Natural Numbers

I tune in to the British Parliament channel to hear:

> Mr. Speaker, Mr. Speaker, Mr. Speaker ... I, I, I ... I have
> to say to him, I have to say to him, I have to say to him ...

Some of us have an inherent, naturally resonant number in our vocal patterns and behavioral tics. We habitually clear our throats or tap our fingers a certain number of times before speaking. When rituals like these reach a certain level, psychiatrists call it obsessive-compulsive disorder. In fact, the low-key compulsions we will talk about here stem less from illness or neurosis than from something most of us are rather good at: *pattern recognition*.

Once upon a time, those ancestors of ours who were able to spot the outline of a predator in the grass ahead and to take evasive action were more likely to survive (and become our ancestors) than those who couldn't (and didn't). Today, the brain will still produce a small shot of a pleasure-related neurotransmitter like dopamine whenever we notice, consciously or not, a pattern amongst the chaos – whenever we get it right. What self-affirming information might a pattern of three hold for our parliamentary speaker?

"I like the number five," one client told me. "Ever since I noticed that all the flowers on the wallpaper in the loo had five petals. Some days I look everywhere for fives." You could say that the compulsive Emergent Knowledge facilitator sees everything in sixes, but that would not be entirely true. Sometimes we see them in multiples of six.

Grove called our patterns of vocal and behavioral tics, and other forms of natural numbers, 'Clean Answers' – response-related utterances unmediated by conscious thought. They invariably held information that a facilitator could help the client release without recourse to anything too complicated. You will recall Julia, the businesswoman in Part Five, half-consciously filing away something that she had learned about herself:

> Hm. Hm. Hm.

What could be coded in Clean Answers like these?

> *And what does that first hm know?*
> *And the second?*
> *And the third?*

Julia's first, she came to recognize, held a deep knowing; the second protected that knowing; and the third – which, like the others, offered its information only when prompted – confirmed the first and second. A pattern of three that was self-reinforcing. A pattern of four might have signaled doubt or uncertainty; five, pain or dismay; six, an epiphany. I am speculating. There is more work to be done here.

The Ordinal Six

Occasionally David and I would debate the ideal setting for an Emergent Knowledge procedure. We finally agreed that there were two kinds: one a rigorously neutral space containing as little sensory distraction as possible; the other wherever you happened to be at the time.

In the fall of 2007, we find ourselves in a hotel lobby in Paris, discussing a preliminary paper on the Power of Six with colleagues (Figure 44).

Figure 44. Left to right: the author, Grove, Brenda, Silvie de Clerck

One of them, BRENDA, a clinical psychologist, is about to offer me feedback. She leans forward slightly and says:

The first thing I noticed ...

Before she can complete the thought, David matches her with a micro-movement of his own:

And the second thing?

'First', 'second', and so on are ordinal numbers identifying the sequencing of an ordered set. If there is a first thing, there has to be a second and *a priori* more. The ordinal imperative Brenda has introduced draws attention not only to the importance of the first thing she noticed, but also to the fact that she noticed other things too. Equally of interest to the facilitator at this particular moment is the information coded in the unconscious nonverbal Brenda used to accompany her words – that little lean forward – and the crisp tone of voice she used. She responds to David's "And the second thing?" with:

Hm. I sensed a certain abruptness.

And the third thing?
(Her eyes roll to the sky in recognition) I'm reminded of my mother.

And the fourth thing?

And the fifth and sixth. The facilitator is following a precondition that the client herself has introduced. Meanwhile, Brenda finds herself working her way through the relationship she had with her mother and a little while later ends on a new learning – as a result of which her feedback on the paper is not abrupt at all, but rather gentle. I should point out that Brenda knew David of old. In any other context, the involuntary client might have flattened the self-appointed therapist before things had gone so far.

The information that manifests in a little move or a murmur will last a very short time and might seem insignificant, but just as a small change can make a considerable difference to a person's life, a small move and a few modest questions can too.

'The Ordinal Six,' or as we would sometimes call it, 'Running the Numbers,' is a simple heuristic derived from this intervention. The facilitator has no need to wait for a clue to be supplied by the client, but can go in without any preliminaries:

What is the first thing? or
What is the first thing you know?

The respondent will normally direct the question to an issue that is taking their attention at the time. Whatever the response, the facilitator will follow up, inevitably, with:

And what is the second thing?
And what is the third thing?
And the fourth thing?
And the fifth?
And sixth?

Given a reasonable level of rapport, the wording of the question can be gradually reduced, distancing the facilitator even further from the scene. Facilitators in any doubt about their ability to do that, however, should stick to the full syntax. Either way, as in any Clean process, *the respondent is under no obligation to explain or to elaborate their response.*

In a conventional counseling situation, the client has little choice but to translate the language of the counselor into subjective meaning and to reply in language that must then be re-translated by the counselor in turn. Something is always lost (or mistakenly gained) in translation. Both parties to the exchange create a personal version of what the other has said which may well be at odds with the version intended. This can be very frustrating for those whose lives from beginning to end are predicated on seeking out, creating, and communicating meaning. The same words and symbols mean different things to different people, and meaning may continually shift for the person concerned.

Mostly we cope with the misunderstandings that result by allowing a certain amount of slack and keeping our communication expectations low, but when expectations are high – in business, say, or the law, or in the early years of the average marriage – stress levels will rise to meet them.

The Ordinal Six makes ample allowance for differing meanings and shifting meanings, and it does so in a particular way, as we see in the example below.

MARGARET is a medical practitioner who has been working on a problem she has been aware of for years: the conflict between "getting on with things" and "stopping to think." I have no inclination to ask Margaret what she means by these expressions. She is not, after all, using language to reveal, but to represent, her experience. Instead, I ask:

> *What is the first thing you know about that?*
> Eh? Well, that ... no ... well it's as if there are so many things, I'm not sure which I want.

> *And what is the second thing?*
> Often I make a decision and just do something rather than hang around.

And what is the third thing?
I know that sometimes it comes back and hits you because
it wasn't well thought out.

The cryptic constructs Margaret is using ("so many things,"
"sometimes," "hang around," "hits you") are likely to have
multiple meanings for her and the meanings may be continually
shifting. I could quiz her at length and in some detail about this
omnium gatherum of semantic possibilities. As the critic John
Ruskin said, it is not too difficult to be complicated. Or I can
deliver a simple procedure that allows natural ambiguity,
multiplicity, and diversity of meaning to co-exist in the client
while she gets on with sorting out priorities in the way that only
she can.

Margaret has no need to attempt to explain to me what she
means by her expressions and metaphors; nor does she have to
limit herself to a single meaning; and nor does she have to
conform to some assumption of shared meaning, a semantic trap
that would have her constantly adjusting *her* meaning to what she
supposed *mine might be,* thereby opening up potential chasms of
misunderstanding that could swallow us both. The Ordinal Six will
self-sort meaning for the client in her own terms and in her own
time.

And what is the fourth thing?
Hm, there are times and places for thinking that are NOT
the times and places for decisive action.

And what is the fifth thing?
It's like that saying, "There are some things you can do
something about and some things you can't," and
sometimes I don't know which is which and it gets very
messy.

And what is the sixth thing?
Ah, just relaxing and letting things happen.

The client began with an unsatisfying feeling whose 'meaning' for
her has shifted from:

uncertainty ("I'm not sure whether to"), to
impatience ("I just do something rather than ..."), to
self-doubt ("it wasn't well thought out"), to
equivocation ("Hm ..." etc.), to
confusion and despair ("sometimes I don't know which
is which and it gets very messy").

And yet out of these shifting sands has emerged a positive sense of:

relaxation ("and just letting things happen").

And now *what do you know?*
I can plan, and learn, and leave it be.

Meaning has changed again, to *permission* and *possibility.*

The Ordinal Six will benefit from further research. On some occasions, it has proved sufficient in itself and useful information has emerged. At other times, it has thrown up information that was pursued in other ways. Meanwhile, I believe it is the very starkness of the questioning and the simplicity of the discipline that are its strengths. What seems to happen is that the initial intervention ("What is the first thing?") switches on the system's iterative engine, so that by the time the client's mental gears are engaged, the unconscious is already primed. This can accelerate systemic learning in a way that conventional questioning based on the *interpretation and discussion of meaning* cannot.

It may be difficult at times to be simple, but it is not all that complicated.

§

Part Six Emerging

Chapter 3
Witnesses

The more a story is told, the more it improves.   Anon

The original sense of 'improve' was 'increase the value of.' Our natural inclination to add value in telling and re-telling a story inspired this self-organizing application of the Power of Six. The idea behind it is that the central essentials of a client's narrative will survive, while anything obsolete or of doubtful value will be discarded or subsumed. Intrinsic worth advances, inessentials fall by the wayside.

The client is piloted through a number of sessions using Clean or Emergent questioning. At any time, but particularly if the issue seems to be stuck fast, the client can be invited to present what they know to someone who has not been privy to the process. The facilitator briefs the witness to listen to the client supportively *without question or comment*. At the end, the witness asks one thing only:

And now *what do you know?*

The client responds, the witness leaves, the facilitator sends in a second witness and the client tells their story again as if for the first time. This sequence is followed six times. It is a new slant on that old definition of a good conversation: a monologue delivered in the presence of others.

A necessary, though limiting, condition of the exercise is that six witnesses should be available as and when required. There is a debate about whether the witnesses should be strangers to the client or not, or even if they should understand the client's language. My own view on both questions is that it does not matter.

Another condition is that the exercise should be continuous, reducing the chances of the narrative being affected by events outside the narrator's control. Any 'improvement' in the story will thus be the result of an internal decision by the client and emerge from the world of the story itself. More research is needed here.

At the end of the sixth witnessing, the facilitator returns to ask the client the difference question:

> *And what is the difference between what you knew at the*
> *start and what you know now?*

JUDY is a company director trying to get a business project off the ground with a group of associates. She describes the situation as rather like being in a hovercraft that is ready to take off, except that two members of the crew are keeping it tethered to the ground with ropes. Judy is impatient for the two crew either to let go the ropes and get on board or to wave the hovercraft and the project goodbye.

I accompany Judy through a standard Power of Six process based on a drawing she does of her metaphor, then send in witness #1. Judy tells her story succinctly using the drawing. She tells the story again to witnesses #2, #3, #4, and #5, and with each telling her description of the hovercraft and its recalcitrant crew develops in some small but significant particular that reflects her growing impatience with the real-life situation.

By the fifth ('crash and burn') telling, she is ready to cut the ropes holding the hovercraft, a radical move that would have the effect of leaving the two crew behind. But during her sixth ('out of the ashes') account, a critical component of the narrative changes, and at the end when I ask Judy the difference question, it is clear that value has accrued not only to the advantage of the narrator, but also to the system of which the narrator is a part. Judy reports:

> I had a shiny new metaphor at the start and it was moving
> almost unstoppably, but at the end I knew a lot more about
> myself and my relationships to the other people involved,

and how that relates to the energy the project needs. It reminds me of making a sales pitch, and after each call we would stop and consider what we knew now and on the next pitch adjust it accordingly. Only this isn't about sales, it's about taking into account the different energies and strengths of other people.

An observation that echoes one of the key features of emergence, the 'taking into account' effect of the different energies of the numbers in iterative progression.

ROB McGAVOCK is a therapist who knew David Grove as friend and mentor for many years. As a result of their work together, Rob obtained significant relief from what he describes as "a very primitive and infantile trauma that had never been touched by conventional therapy." At the time I met Rob, he had not been able to tie up all the loose ends as he would have wished. "I think David found me a tough nut to crack," Rob told me. He joked that he was waiting for David to get good enough to heal him. Then something different happened. In Rob's own words:

> It was the Power of Six that did the trick. David was constantly using me and others as willing test subjects. In my case, this time he began with a Power of Six session on the gyroscope as a warm up and that seemed to loosen me up psychologically and emotionally.

I witnessed Rob's process that day. He was inspired to map out a complete panorama of his life, including all the elements that had been revealed in his work with David over the years. At the end, he had eight pieces of flipchart paper taped together and hung out in the garden. David then did something he had never done before.

> He had me tell this entire story of my life to six different people, one of whom barely understood English. When I finished with one, he would send along another. What mattered was that I was telling my story to six different witnesses, each time as for the first time. In the process, something began to happen. It is really hard to describe. It was very subtle, yet powerful. My story began to

abbreviate. Elements that were dysfunctional and had persisted simply began to expire. I could feel it happening, but I couldn't describe it. It was one of the most powerful, yet at the same time gentle, healing experiences that have ever occurred for me.

A year after this session, Rob tells me he feels a freedom he has never felt before. His life is more peaceful, he feels less encumbered, and he breathes more easily. The only constraints left, he says, are the ones that are self-imposed and resolvable.

A key feature of iteration and emergence is that they build on whatever has gone before. Company coach Lynne Burney uses a variation of the witnessing exercise in her corporate training. Participants tell their success story of the year separately to six colleagues in preparation for shared vision or creative work that looks to the future.

In an extension of the psychotherapeutic application of the formula, I imagine taking a group of dedicated participants, with or without any history of therapy, through six re-tellings of their lives in the expectation of self-healing. This week-long exercise in Emergent Self Knowledge would be a little different from the therapist directed 're-storying' of White and Epston's narrative therapy (see the References). My version would take place over six days on a Greek island, say, with the seventh a day of rest for clients to consider "And now what do you know?" while sunbathing or snorkeling.

White and Epston, by the way, identify a number of key conversations that need to take place between therapist and client before change can come about using their methods, and it so happens – well, you guessed – there are six of them.

§

Part Six Emerging

Chapter 4
Teams: Teambuilding
The Six-Sided Table

Great things are not done by impulse, but by a series of small things brought together.   Vincent van Gogh

Teambuilding

What is the definition of a perfect marriage? It is not when the perfect couple come together, but when the imperfect couple learn to enjoy their differences.

Here is an application of Emergent Knowledge at the interface between metaphor, sixness, and witnessing. It will help a new team coming together for the first time or an existing team seeking renewal. The exercise developed from the internal workings of our Clean Research Group, which meets several times a year for a day devoted to research into Clean Language, Metaphor, and Emergence related topics. Occasionally, we ask a new person if they would like to join the group. The question we put to them prior to their first visit is:

> *The kind of research group you would like to belong to is like what?*

The person is invited to bring a metaphor, usually in the form of a drawing, and to present it to the group. We discuss the metaphor (not the person), take on the parts we like and negotiate parts we don't. What used to happen then is that we would integrate key features of the metaphor into a consensual metaphor landscape we had drawn and developed over the years.

The procedure worked well enough when the Clean community was a close one and we were recruiting from people most of us knew. But as the community grew, new candidates were finding it increasingly difficult to relate to the old metaphor and eventually it was consigned to the archive. After that, there was more discussion than usual about what we liked and didn't like about new members' metaphors. Emotional and conceptual gaps began to appear, and after a while the question, 'Do we still have a common purpose?' was raised.

In the absence of the old group metaphor as a benchmark, we went back to basics: "The kind of research group you would like to belong to is like what?" we asked ourselves, and came up with "It's like a voyage to an unknown island," "Colors of the rainbow merging together," "Multiple dimensions in space," "Synchronized swimming", and so on. Even a cursory analysis of these revealed very different, unconsciously derived constructs that affected the way we participated in the group, colored our views of other members, and shaped our beliefs and assumptions about the group's objectives and methods. We discussed what to do with this information, and rather than agree on a procedure for eliciting a new group metaphor, something surprising emerged.

I have generalized the teambuilding exercise we came up with into this six-step mix of individual metaphor, Clean Language, the Power of Six, and 'witnessing'.

> 1 Members of the team pair off. One elicits a metaphor from the other: "For you working in a team [or in this team or on this project] is like what?" *The elicitor/witness does not comment on the metaphor and there is no discussion or negotiation around it.* The witness may ask a couple of Clean questions to help the respondent clarify the metaphor for themself. The roles are then reversed and the same procedure is followed.

Members of our group (therapists, counselors, coaches, researchers, trainers) found it significantly easier to talk to each other at a metaphorical, rather than at an emotional or cognitive, level about their purpose for the group and their perceived role in it. And we appreciated the (unique) opportunity to talk without interruption or challenge or, indeed, any comment at all.

2 New pairs form. As before, one describes their metaphor for the group or team in some detail and is witnessed *without comment*. The witness may ask one or two Clean questions to clarify the metaphor. The roles are then reversed.

We noticed that in the new pairings, one person's metaphor would often incorporate an element of another's *from the previous pairing*. For some of us it was easier to allow the influence of another if it was to a third person and couched in symbolic rather than directly personal terms.

3 Pairings change again. The same procedure is followed. Pairings change until every individual has presented their metaphor to another person *six times in all*.

4 The group reconvenes. Members share their experience.

5 The group facilitator asks everyone the 'difference' question and responses are shared in the group.

6 Further iterations may be followed as time and inclination allow until the facilitator brings proceedings to a conclusion, or the team agrees, "That's it."

Given reasonable goodwill, a merging of some elements of members' individual metaphors is to be expected. However, and crucially, there is *no expectation* on people to modify their metaphors. The object of the exercise is not to negotiate a shared metaphor (though the exercise could be adapted for this), but to have individual metaphors elicited and witnessed *six times over.* During this time, individuals may amend or develop their metaphors as they wish.

At the end of the exercise, people spoke of a "broadening out" of their awareness of each other. As one participant said, "There is a coming together of the group in a subtler way. The team becomes a commonality of individuality. It is a subtle, powerful process."

Our team is still together, by the way, after twelve years.

The Six-Sided Table

In 1990, the National Theatre of Great Britain commissioned the playwright David Edgar to write a play following the transition of an unnamed Eastern European state from totalitarian rule to democracy. Its title, *The Shape of the Table*, referred to meetings between the Americans and Vietnamese during the Vietnam War, when the delegations spent months discussing the literal shape of the negotiating table.

Some years later, Grove began asking, "What would happen if client and problem could be induced to sit at the table together and play out their cards simultaneously?" I for one had no idea. Then he met Lynne Burney, who had spent years getting rid of tables in business meetings on the grounds that they interfered with direct communications between people. Burney immediately picked up on the idea of management and employees laying all their cards on the table, and supposed that if the resulting information could be iterated intelligently in some way, a positive outcome would emerge. Perhaps the table itself could be induced to give up what it knew. What kind of table would do that?

Well, in 2007 or so, it became obvious that it had to be a six-sided table. And if real six-sided tables were not too easy to come by, they could be metaphorically six-sided: round, square, or oblong, but each having, as we shall see, six parts.

Burney designed and ran the following exercise for forty medical professionals in a large pharmaceutical company. The aim was to activate an energetic response to radical organizational changes that were to be announced at the start of a three-day conference. No negotiation of the changes would be possible. The expectation of the team leader was that forty polite professionals would never be able to say what they felt in the circumstances. Burney's job was to ensure that they did just that.

Here is a participant's view of what happened. The changes have just been explained and people are feeling what they are feeling – resistant, fearful, angry, curious, excited. A huge range of emotions is bubbling below the corporate surface.

1 I am at a table with five other people. We are given six large green envelopes containing a sheet of paper divided into six parts. My neighbors at the five other tables have similar envelopes. "You are going to be asked a question," we are told, "and we would like you to write your response anonymously in the space at the top of the paper, then place the paper back in the envelope."

2 The question is "What is happening for you now in this new organization?" I write down what I am feeling (uncertain). When time is called, we are asked to take our envelopes to another table and leave them randomly. There is a buzz in the air. It's fun to move around.

3 Back at my table I find the envelopes that others have left. We are asked virtually the same question: "And what else is happening for you now in this new organization?" I take one of the envelopes, write my response (which isn't very different) in the second space of the new sheet of paper, place it back in the envelope, and when time is called, deliver the envelope randomly to another table.

4 The same procedure. We respond to the same question a third, fourth, fifth, and sixth time on different sheets of paper. On the fourth occasion, I hear a few frustrated voices. Some of the comments I read later are on the lines of, "I don't know," "My competence is not being fully utilized," and "Now I am getting angry at this childish repetition." The fifth time: "People dare to say what they think!" "There appears to be a lot of unhappiness," "Communications need to be worked on," "Some people are disappointed and need reassurance."

5 The final question is, "And *now* what do you know?" We write our responses.

6 We come back together in a plenary session to debrief.

Having talked over the results of this exercise with Lynne Burney in some detail, I believe that one of the benefits of the experiment is that it did not come off as smoothly as corporate communications are normally supposed to. It brought the obstacles to change into the open – a risky and at times uncomfortable thing to do, but a problem shared is one less to be feared. The learning for Lynne was to trust the process:

> As facilitator, I had to be willing to step into the fire. The Power of Six for me lies in allowing you to go through the negatives while trusting that something positive will emerge. Getting to the obstacles and getting through them brings clarity to the system and allows you to move on. The final download question, "And now what do you know?", is important, because it allows people time to seize the essence of the experience.

Employees used the shared experience as an emotional touchstone when it came to discussing and implementing the changes. The exercise itself may not have been as much fun as participants had hoped, but as Mae West once said, you can't always be funny when you have to be clean.

§

Part Six Emerging

Chapter 5
Reflections

*Mirrors would do well to reflect a little more before
sending back images.* Jean Cocteau

A reflection does more than reproduce an image. It throws back
light and heat on the thing reflected. Reflection is one of the means
by which the mind comes to know itself.

The client is invited to look at themself in a full-length mirror.
The facilitator asks:

What do you know? or
What is the first thing you know?

followed by the usual corollaries. At the end of the process, one
client reported:

I responded as if I were looking at myself quite differently.
I was led to areas that were very new for me.

Another:

It took me to a different level that I was not expecting to go.

A three-way mirror enables clients to view themselves from the
back and sides too. Three separate mirrors, one a hand mirror that
can be easily manipulated, offer more possibilities still. My
colleague WENDY was a research volunteer for the three-mirror
exercise:

I really liked having the multiple perspectives available to
me, particularly that provided by the hand mirror. I don't

generally do a lot of looking back in my life, and it may be a good idea to do more. At the start of the exercise, I was answering the questions by reflecting on my hair and clothes, but by the end, I was thinking quite deeply about perspectives in relation to different patterns that run through my life. It was a fairly comprehensive difference.

In terms of the standard set up (client at A, problem at B, space between of C), the client at A is viewing their image at a B that is actually an A once removed, and there is a sense of both a real and perceived space of C between them. Every one of these parallel worlds can be questioned separately to reveal what it knows.

Clean Reflections also makes for an engaging exercise in couples counseling. The partners have implicit permission to scrutinize each other and themselves as a pair more objectively when the gaze is, as here, indirect.

An occasionally hilarious variation invites clients to use props and costume to explore aspects of themselves that are not normally on view. Hats and masks in particular can have a galvanizing effect. The 'neutral' mask, for example, enables the wearer to project almost any state they are minded to explore (Figure 45).

happy   sad

Figure 45. Clean reflections

One volunteer thought very carefully about this exercise and decided to don one of her husband's old sweaters. She elected to answer the questions silently to herself, so all I know about her process is what she reported at the end:

Such simple questions. Such a lot of learning.

§

Part Six Emerging

Chapter 6
Prescriptions: Written
Emailed
Online

The simple is the seal of the true. Latin proverb

"Patients are walking in off the street," David would say after one of our busier days at the medical center, "and after a few minutes we can say to them, 'Put that on paper, ask yourself six times what else could go on there, we'll be back.'" After a number of brief encounters like this, we came up with the idea of prescriptions.

The word 'prescription' means something that has been 'written before'. In each of the applications in this chapter, the Power of Six questions are available to the client in advance.

Written

We are working with a young couple who are having some success in coming off drugs. At the end of several rounds of questioning, we have to leave temporarily, and David suggests to the couple that they take themselves through another round by asking the questions of each other. I write up a basic exercise for them to follow.

When the four of us come back together for a final joint session – yes, I know – it is evident that the couple got on well with the exercise. They are well motivated and keen to support each other. As the session comes to an end, David notices a blank prescription pad on the consulting room desk. He scribbles on it, hands the paper to the couple, and invites them to extend the therapeutic alliance they have established by continuing to work on the issue at home. The prescription reads:

> *What do you know? x 1*
> *And what else do you know? x 5*
> *And now what do you know? x 1*
> *Repeat x 6*

The exact wording of a prescription like this would vary according to the needs of the client or clients at the time. It might be geared to questioning B or C rather than A, or to moving, or turning, or to self-facilitating a Clean Start. There would be a note at the end suggesting a follow-up appointment to develop what had been learned from the exercise or to request a repeat prescription.

Emailed

Here is an electronic version of the same idea. DANIEL is a therapist who works from a model combining NLP and Clean Language. He emails me from another country:

> I have been asked to help 'G', a 17-year old with emotional, behavioral, and learning difficulties who has been to a number of psychologists and psychiatrists. This morning he was kicked out of his father's home because of his lies, theft, and disruptive behavior. It looks as if he will end up on the street or in jail, where he will most likely be raped, infected with Aids, and lost to crime. My initial response is to run very far from him. Do you have any ideas or suggestions?

Once upon a time, I would have been nonplussed over a request like this (now I might just be at sixes and sevens). I would have been concerned about my own expertise, I would have looked up the precedents, I would have consulted colleagues. In fact, all I have to do is determine one thing: who is asking whom for what? Whoever has asked Daniel for help ("I have been asked to help G," he says) has not asked for mine. And G, who is neither my client nor Daniel's, does not appear to have asked for anything.

I reproduce my correspondence with Daniel as an application of the Power of Six to distance learning territory. My first response to his email is, "What is it you want from writing to me?" Daniel replies:

> To ensure that I am the best person to help G out of his destructive patterns and to heal his past. And to get help for myself first, as I feel out of my depth.

Already we see a shift of emphasis. Daniel began with the assumption that he should help G, and although he is still attached to this, he now acknowledges that he must first help himself. I respond:

> *I'm going to ask six more questions. I suggest you answer them in turn, without looking at the next question until you have answered the current one. Type in your response to each question.*

I leave a space between each. The message I receive in reply is transcribed below. The structural analysis – 'proclaim', 'explain', etc. – I added later.

> 1 *What do you know about your response to my first question?*
> I believe that there are a number of psychological and pathological problems hidden in this young man, and I have a feeling of inadequacy about helping him.
> [proclaim]

> 2 *And what else do you know?*
> That I should most likely walk away from this as I have not had any experience in this area and I am not proficient enough in Clean Language.
> [explain]

> 3 *And what else do you know?*
> When I feel overwhelmed and unsure of myself and my competence, I read and think more instead of just getting on with the task and trusting myself.
> [reinforce]

> 4 *And what else do you know?*
> I'm trying to convince myself that it will be okay to work

with G, and I want someone to confirm that or tell me to get the heck away, because I could have a massive negative effect on him and aggravate the situation.   [the wobble]

Daniel's replies show someone following a typical Power of Six response pattern, even though the questions to which he is responding were available to him (if he chose) in advance.

5 *And what else do you know?*
If G is really ready and desperate to change he will, HOWEVER he may not be ready or willing! [crash and burn]

6 *And what else do you know?*
No matter what happens or does not happen, all I can do is be available to help, while G will need to take responsibility to do what he can to get the help he needs.
[out of the ashes]

6+1 *And* now *what do you know?*
I have a strong desire to master Clean Language to help G and others.   [learning]

I guess that Daniel hasn't gone quite where he expected to go, but he has ended up where he needed to be (and not a bad place at that). A few days later, he writes to tell me that G has been admitted to a rehab facility, which solves Daniel's immediate problem of whether to take him on as a client or not. In fact, Daniel had already answered that conundrum for himself by accepting [#5] that G "may not be ready or willing to change" and [#6] that he "will need to take responsibility to get the help he needs."

In other words, if the right questions are asked, the right answers lie *with no one but the respondent*, which in this case is neither G nor whoever asked Daniel to help G, but Daniel himself.

When I last saw David, he talked about producing a set of pre-printed cards that would free highly motivated clients like Daniel, Silvie, and the young couple at the clinic from unnecessary 'projection' and 'transference' by replacing the therapist altogether.

David's former assistant Matthew Hudson has fulfilled this intention, though in a way that David had not anticipated.

Online

Matthew has created an online version of an Emergent Self Knowledge prescription at the powersofsix.com website. 'The Iterator' guides visitors through a set of standard procedures (including one or two variants on those in this book) and if requested emails them a copy. Many people have kindly forwarded their processes to me for research purposes. I was particularly struck by this record of an online session sent by a psychiatrist who works at a health center in Uttar Pradesh, India. DR. RAJ JOSHI was concerned about a particular patient who came to him suffering from obsessive-compulsive disorder.

An on-screen box invites Dr. Joshi to type in what he would like to work on. He writes:

> How to help a young man suffering from OCD.

He clicks on 'Next'. Up comes the question,

> *What do you know about that?*   [#1]

Dr. Joshi types:

> This is a very difficult case, as his obsessive-compulsive symptoms are quite resistant to pharmacotherapy and counseling.
>
> *And what else do you know about that?*   [#2]
> The patient's father has an attitude of dissatisfaction and blaming the professionals for lack of improvement in the patient.
>
> *And what else do you know about that?*   [#3]
> The patient himself wants to talk a lot, but has low tolerance for his OC symptoms.
>
> *And what else do you know about that?*   [#4]
> He desperately wants to get rid of his problem and so does the father.

And what else do you know about that?   [#5]
Apart from pharmacotherapy, what works is for someone
to be constantly in communication with the patient in order
for him to feel comfortable and have relief from his
symptoms.

And what else do you know about that?   [#6]
The patient is in the grip of conflicting messages from his
religious exposure and internal hedonistic desires.

And now *what do you know?*   [learning]
I need to get at the roots of the patient's difficulties by
entering into a dialogue with him without getting frustrated
by my lack of progress with his symptoms.

*And what is the difference between what you knew at the
start and what you know now?*   [difference]
What I thought was the patient's problem – his lack of
tolerance for his symptoms – is also a problem with his
father and with my own self. And that is a revelation as
well as a handle for me to work upon further!

I ask Dr. Joshi to say more about what he has learned and the
difference it has made to his work. His reply highlights the extent
to which *his own* and *the patient's father's* problems (impatience
and intolerance) were reflected in the persistence of *the patient's*
problem (a constant need for attention and reassurance). Authority
and dependency figures were caught in a vicious circle.

It was a key systemic learning that Dr. Joshi tells me he takes
into his work with every other patient he sees. His counseling
skills, he says, have much improved.

Finally, here are excerpts from another online process that begins
unexceptionally, but develops in a way that perhaps says all there
is to say about self-determination and emergent self knowledge.

EDUARDO is a futures trader who is not too happy with his life.

Type in something you would like to work on.
I don't enjoy how I earn money.

What do you know about that?
That it's boring, unfulfilling, and somewhat pointless.
I'm gaining no worthwhile skills from it.

And what else do you know about that?

And so on. His response to the fourth iteration of the first round is:

That my time could be put to better use.

To the sixth:

That happiness comes from doing what I enjoy.

His learning at the end of the first round is:

That I need to do what interests me and what I enjoy.

And the difference between what he knew at the start and what he knows now?

I need to shift my focus from what I don't like onto what
I do. Thanks for this Iterator thing! ☺

So far, so good. For some people, a single round that takes them to a place like this will be as far as they need to go. But something continues to niggle Eduardo. He has uncovered a need "to shift focus," but no idea of where to shift it or how. The next day he returns to the computer and takes himself through a second round. His learning at the end has a much wider frame of reference:

That it's an ongoing process of knowing, unraveling, and
reconstructing and so on. Improving being human.

The question of *what he does* has been subsumed into *who he is*, a bigger picture altogether. Eduardo's initial purpose is receding, while his "ongoing process of knowing" evolves:

Round #3 learning after another set of six
I know I can do this. This is who I am.

Round #4 learning
I feel like I've arrived somewhere new. I'm excited by
the possibilities.

> *Round #5 learning*
> I feel like I'm coming home after a long absence. It is
> totally new, but somehow home.
>
> *Round #6 learning*
> I have changed somewhat. ☺ It's like there is a universe
> inside me and it's the same as the one outside me.

What you see here are the edited highlights of Eduardo's progress.
I have left most of his work – the fluffed lines, retakes, and
repetitive bits – on the cutting room floor. But you can imagine the
dedication and drive required by this client to get through six
rounds of self-regulated repetition, iteration, and recursion to
arrive at a state where the "universe inside" is the same as "the one
outside." A model 'integration' analogy. The program now asks:

> *And what is the difference between what you knew at the
> start and what you know now?*
> That I am one and the same thing as my constructs. I am
> the architect of my reality, the meaning-maker of my
> existence. Wow! This is cool and bizarre. Hmm, lots of
> musing to do. ☺

Good as far as it goes. I wish every one of us the recognition that
we are the architects and meaning-makers of our existence, but I
find myself wondering if Eduardo has *achieved* the model of
integration to which he aspired, or is only able to *conceive* of it.
He admits that he still has "lots of musing" to do. If we look back
at his round #6 learning, we can see that although he said he had
"changed", he slipped in a modest little modifier, "somewhat".
And note that "*like* there is a universe ..." This could be, like, old
hippie slang, but it begs the question: is there a universe inside him
that is the same as the one outside or not? A thing that is like
something is not the thing itself.

   Little linguistic indicators of doubt are not too difficult to pick
up in a live exchange when our ears are attuned to them. A
conscientious Clean Language investigator would be expected to
detain suspects like "somewhat", "like", "hmm" and "musing" and
interrogate them on the spot, if only to eliminate them from their
enquiries. The Emergent Knowledge inquirer hears reservations

and evasions differently. The Power of Six patterns are such that equivocation of any kind by the client will be translated into bodymind signals that may be resisted, or defied, or filed for consideration later, but will not go away. When you have experienced the process for yourself, you will know what I mean.

A week after his six rounds, Eduardo returns to the Iterator and begins where he left off. In reply to "What would you like to work on?" he types:

> I am my own construct, and I can make my construct
> anything I like – once I figure it out.

So yes, still musing. His self-examination continues. The program now comes up with a variant on the earlier questions:

> *And what does that know about you?*

Eduardo proclaims his response: his construct knows that he's doing pretty well.

> *And what else does that know about you?*

He explains that he's changed just the way he needed to. The same question. He reinforces his position. The same again. Only now does he experience another slight, but unequivocal, wobble:

> A little doubt-space may still be there. I'm not yet
> thoroughly transformed.

And at the same, fourth, place in rounds eight and nine:

> It's not as solid as I'd hoped. It seems not to have fully
> percolated through to my outermost reaches.

> I'm changing in a desirable way, though there's more work
> to be done, sadly.

Eduardo has been telling himself he is getting on well, yet the signals have persisted: "It's not as solid as," "It seems not to have," "there's more." They are urging him to go further. He sets out again. And at the end of round ten:

> It's much more peaceful and complete. I'm happy now.
> Big sigh of relief.

I am just about to sigh in relief with him, when he adds:

> Though there's always something more. ☺

I can almost see the rueful smile on Eduardo's face as he acknowledges that he is not yet *fully* complete. He finds himself embarking on another round, his eleventh, and at the fourth iteration recognizes what that "something more" is:

> My emotional inconsistencies and weaknesses.

An unexpected obstacle. The relentless persistence of the Power of Six has finally laid bare a symptom that hitherto, I suspect, has been very well protected. For a moment, the client is overwhelmed by the apparent size and complexity of this barrier to progress. He clicks on the next question.

> *And what else do you know?*

Complexity collapses suddenly. In an epiphanic insight, Eduardo acknowledges his prolonged and private feelings of conflict and frailty for what they are: merely human. Not peculiar, not contemptible, not something to lock away in shame or deny. And in a twelfth climactic round, he is able to confront and conquers his worst fears about himself. Out of the ashes of his inconsistencies and weaknesses comes the recognition that:

> I'm whole, peaceful, and protected, *and also fully open.*
> I can't believe I haven't done this before.

It may not quite be the end, but it is a good ending. The Maori say that twelve is the number of stars that we try to reach and touch during our journey through life. Twelve and multiples of twelve are the numbers for all the trails of the sea, the land, the mind, and the spirit. Eduardo's twelve trails may seem like a long journey to him in terms of how far he has come therapeutically, yet they consisted of only eighty-six steps: twelve set-up, sixty iterative, twelve learning, and two difference questions and responses.

The client signs off with the thought that:

> It's so elegant, it's perfectly balanced, it has self-sustaining sustainability. This is opening up whole new vistas of being and doing. I have a changed felt sense of myself.

With a percipient "*is* opening up," Eduardo acknowledges that even a changed felt sense is an ongoing state. He continues, as do we all, to emerge.

§

The Iterator was developed after David had left us, but is very much in his mode. He would have embraced its self-prescriptive, facilitator-free form as he did his friends, with open arms and unqualified delight. A wholly self-regulated process will not meet the needs of every client, of course, because it requires a high degree of discipline, persistence, and patience, and some clients will always prefer to work with a facilitator directly. Yet when written, emailed, or self-dispensed prescriptions work, they work brilliantly, enabling people to answer their existential doubts and difficulties for themselves. Which was, after all, Grove's life purpose, and is the self-determining, self-empowering purpose of every exercise of the Power of Six in these pages.

Two thousand and more years ago, the seven sages of ancient Greece met in the Temple of Apollo at Delphi to agree on a body of common knowledge for inscribing there. The first and most enduring of their precepts was the plain but profound principle that inspires this book: *Know thyself*. This extraordinary challenge to us all continues to echo down the ages. My aim here has been to *proclaim* it anew, to *explain* it, to *reinforce* its message, and to document a few *wobbles* and *crashes* on the way to what, I trust, will be the emergence of new knowledge and learning. That, and to add a few numbers to the sum of human happiness.

Post Script

You might like to ask yourself:

What is the difference between what I knew at the start and what I know now?

References and Further Reading

There are a number of theoretical and practical underpinnings to Emergent Self Knowledge and the Power of Six that you might find it useful to familiarize yourself with if you haven't done so already.

CLEAN LANGUAGE teaches facilitators how to keep their questioning non-assumptive, non-suggestive, and non-interpretive ('clean') in order to allow clients access to their subjective experience with minimal interference. The thirty or so Clean questions do not introduce ideas to the client, but encourage the client's own model of the world to emerge.

THERAPEUTIC METAPHOR uses Clean questioning to elicit and develop the symbols and metaphors we generate verbally and non-verbally. Symbol and metaphor are the royal route to the unconscious.

INTERGENERATIONAL HEALING utilizes biographical and genealogical information released via Clean Language questioning to generate resources for the relief or resolution of genealogically sourced problems.

SYMBOLIC MODELLING is Tompkins and Lawley's comprehensive model of Grove's work in Clean Language, Therapeutic Metaphor, and Intergenerational Healing.

CLEAN SPACE is a methodology based on the discovery that there is valuable information to be found in the internal and external bodymind spaces clients occupy rather than focusing solely on the linguistic constructions they employ.

SELF-ALIGNMENT is a process modeled by Matthew Hudson on the 'project' work he did with Grove; it brings the principles of Emergence and the Power of Six to the task of assisting clients to evolve and enrich their personal and professional projects.

Together these models comprise a family of techniques overtly aimed at encouraging emergence. They involve no diagnosis or interpretation of the client's content and no authoritative model of the right solution. They proceed from what is known and experienced by the client, not from what is surmised or suggested by the therapist.

This book represents my personal coding of Emergent Self Knowledge and the Powers of Six. It takes David Grove's work further in a few particulars only, but if you want to get nearer the original, visit **www.powersofsix.com** for articles by myself and Matthew Hudson written shortly after David's death. Our intention was to document his coding as nearly as possible without reference to our own. You can also hear David himself explaining some of his concepts and you can try out 'The Iterator'. For other articles, trainings, and information about the world of 'Clean', visit:

www.cleanlanguage.co.uk
www.innovativepathways.net
www.cleanchange.co.uk
www.trainingattention.co.uk
www.cleanforum.com
www.self-alignment.com

www.cleanlanguage.fr
www.apricotisland.co.uk
www.cleancoaching.com
www.clean.org.nz
www.cleanlanguage.pl
www.coachera.com

Below are listed some of the books, articles, and other sources that helped me write *The Power of Six* or are referenced in the text:

ABC Television, *Six Degrees,* drama series 2006; ITV 2008

Andrew Hodges, *One to Nine: The Inner Life of Numbers*, Short Books 2008

Aristotle, *Metaphysics,* 350 BCE, various translations

Association for Psychological Science, *Complex Decision? Don't Think About It*, Science Daily 10 December 2008

Bernd Rohrbach, *Kreativ Nach Regen ('Rules for Creativity'): Method 635, A New Technique for Solving Problems*, Absatzwirtschaft 1 October 1969

Carl Sagan, *The Demon-haunted World: Science as a Candle in the Dark*, Headline 1996

Cei Davies Linn, *The Inherent Logic of Epistemological Metaphors*, workshop and booklet 2008

Chris Frith, *Making Up the Mind: How the Brain Creates our Mental World*, Blackwell 2007

David J. Grove, *unpublished notes and papers* 1990-2007. With Basil Panzer, *Resolving Traumatic Memories: Metaphor and Symbols in Psychotherapy*, Irvington 1989

Duncan Watts, *Collective Dynamics of Small World Networks,* Nature 1998; with Steven Strogatz, *Six Degrees: The Science of a Collective* Age, Norton 2003

Edward de Bono, *Six Thinking Hats: The Power of Focused Thinking,* MICA Management 1985; *Six Frames for Thinking about Information*, Vermilion 2008

Eric Horvitz and Jure Leskovec, *Worldwide Buzz: Planetary-Scale Views on an Instant Messaging Network*, Microsoft Research 2008

First Analysis Institute of Integrative Studies, *Exploring the Personalities of Numbers and Their Possible Role in Guiding Evolution,* Chicago Feb. 2007

Frigyes Karinthy, *Chain-Links,* story in *Everything is Different,* Budapest 1929

Fritjof Capra, *The Web of Life: A New Synthesis of Mind and Matter*, HarperCollins 1996; *The Hidden Connections: A Science for Sustainable Living,* HarperCollins 2002

George Henry Lewes, *The Physical Basis of Mind,* Boston 1877

George Lakoff and Rafael Núñez, *Where Mathematics Comes From: How the Embodied Mind Brings Mathematics into Being,* Basic Books 2000

Graham Lawton, *Mind Tricks: Six Ways to Explore Your Brain*, New Scientist 1 September 2007

Gregory Bateson, *Steps to an Ecology of Mind: Collected Essays in Anthropology, Psychiatry, Evolution and Epistemology,* Chicago 1972

James Lawley and Penny Tompkins, *Metaphors in Mind: Transformation through Symbolic Modelling,* Developing Company Press 2000. *Symbolic Modelling, an Overview* 1997, *What is Emergence?* 2002, *Thinking Networks* 2004, *Iteration Iteration Iteration* 2007; all at cleanlanguage.co.uk

Jean Chevalier and Alain Gheerbrant, *Penguin Dictionary of Symbols* 1996

Jeffrey Goldstein, *Emergence as a Construct,* Emergence volume1 1999

John Bonner Buck and Elizabeth Buck, *Mechanism of Rhythmic Synchronous Flashing of Fireflies,* Science 1968

John Guare, *Six Degrees of Separation,* play script Vintage 1990

John Kleinberg, *Navigation in a Small World,* Nature 2000; *The Small World Phenomenon: An Algorithmic Perspective,* Proceedings of the 32nd Annual ACM Symposium on the Theory of Computing 2000

John von Neumann, *Zur Theorie der Gesellschaftsspiele ('On the Theory of Games of Strategy'),* Mathematicsche Annalen 1928. With Oskar Morgenstern, *Theory of Games and Economic Behavior,* Princeton 1944

Jonah Lehrer, *The Decisive Moment: How the Brain Makes Up Its Mind,* Canongate 2009

Joseph Campbell, *The Hero's Journey,* Harper and Row 1990

Joseph Le Doux, *The Emotional Brain,* Weidenfeld and Nicolson 1998

Kent D. Palmer, *Orienteering in a Clean Meta-system, a Personal Review of a David Grove Spatial Metaphor Workshop,* cleanlanguage.co.uk 2003

Kevin M. Passino et al, *Swarm Cognition in Honey Bees,* Behavioral Ecology and Sociobiology January 2008

Mark Johnson, *The Meaning of the Body: Aesthetics of Human Understanding,* Chicago 2007; with Eric Kandel, *In Search of Memory: the Emergence of a New Science of Mind,* Norton 2006

Martial and Line Rossignol, Roelof Oldeman, Soraya Benzine-Tizroutine, *The Struggle of Life, or The Natural History of Stress and Adaptation,* treemail.nl

Martin Rees, *Just Six Numbers: The Deep Forces That Shape The Universe,* Weidenfeld and Nicolson 1999

Matthew Hudson, *Basic and Advanced Emergent Knowledge formulae,* powersofsix.com 2008

Matthew P. Walker and Robert Stickgold, *Sleep-dependent Learning and Memory Consolidation,* Neuron 30 September 2004

Maurice Brasher, *Tracking Emergence,* ReSource magazine May 2009 and powersofsix.com

Max Maxwell, *The Socratic Method and Its Effect on Critical Thinking,* socraticmethod.net 2007

Max-Planck-Gesellschaft, *Decision-making May Be Surprisingly Unconscious Activity,* Science Daily 15 April 2008

Michael Polanyi, *Personal Knowledge,* Routledge 1958; *The Tacit Dimension,* Doubleday 1966

Michael S. Schneider, *The Beginner's Guide to Constructing the Universe*, Harper 1995

Michael White, *Maps of Narrative Practice*, Norton 200. With David Epston, *Narrative Means to Therapeutic* Ends, Norton 1990

Ngati Kowhai o Waitaha, *Song of Waitaha: Histories of a Nation*, Wharariki Publishing 1994

Nicolai Hartmann, *Neue Wege der Ontologie*, Kohlhammer 1949, tr. Reinhard C. Kuhn as *New Ways of Ontology*, Greenwood Press 1952

Patrick Lynch, terminal illnesses counseling, paradisekids.org.au

Paul Davies, *The Goldilocks Enigma: Why Is the Universe Just Right for Life?* Penguin 2006

Philip Clayton and Paul Davies, editors, *The Re-Emergence of Emergence*, Oxford 2006

Philip Harland, *Trust Me, I'm The Patient: Clean Language, Metaphor and The New Psychology of Change*, Wayfinder Press 2012; *The Six-Fibonacci Series*, ReSource magazine January 2009; with Matthew Hudson: *The Structure of Emergence*, ReSource Feb., June, Oct. 2008; *Six Steps to Emergent Knowledge* and *A Clean Start for the Power of Six*, powersofsix.com

Peter A. Corning, *The Re-Emergence of 'Emergence'*, complexsystems.org 2002

Plato, *Meno*, 380 BCE; *Theaetetus*, 360 BCE; translator Benjamin Jowett, http://classics.mit.edu/Plato

Randy L. Buckner et al, *The Brain's Default Network*, New York Academy of Science March 2008; with Daniel C. Carroll, *Self-Projection and the Brain*, Trends in Cognitive Science February 2007

Richard Bandler and John Grinder, *Reframing: NLP and the Transformation of Meaning*, Real People Press 1983

Richard Dawkins, *The God Delusion*, Bantam Press 2006; editor *The Oxford Book of Science Writing*, Oxford 2008

Richard L. Gregory, editor *The Oxford Companion to the Mind*, Oxford 2001

Robert McGavock, *A Brief Synopsis of A Healing Experience Through the Power of Six*, powersofsix.com 2008

Steven Strogatz, *Sync: The Emerging Science of Spontaneous Order*, Hyperion 2003

Susan Greenfield, *ID: The Quest for Identity in the 21st Century*, Sceptre 2008

Tudor Rickards, *Problem-Solving Through Creative Analysis*, Wiley 1974

University of Rochester, *Our Unconscious Brain Makes the Best Decisions Possible*, Science Daily 29 December 2008

virtusphere.com: *the virtusphere*

Walter J. Freeman, *How Brains Make Up Their Minds*, Weidenfeld and Nicolson 1999

Wikipedia: *the structure of DNA*

zorb.com: *the Zorb ball*

About the Author

Philip Harland is a Clean Language psychotherapist and a film, television, and theater writer and director. He is a leading authority on Emergent Knowledge and the Power of Six, having worked for many years with the originator of the approach, the innovative and highly regarded therapist David Grove. They ran seminars and co-facilitated clients together in Britain, France, and New Zealand. Philip is the author of Trust Me, I'm The Patient and numerous articles on Clean Language and Emergent Knowledge. For more information, visit powersofsix.com and wayfinderpress.co.uk

Index

problem
different kinds of 97-9
eliciting 121-124
exploring 217-220
metaphor for 122
questioning of 146-9
scale of 123-4
solving 206-216
space of B 97-100
unique to individual 227
Proclaim (no. 1) 66-7
prologue event 121-2
props and costume 260
psychogeography 230
psychotherapy and seminars 277
Pythagoras mathematician 57, 66,
68, 72, 82, 84

questioning
ABC system 153-161
Clean Start 121-135, 171-2,
176-9
client moving from A 139-141
client stationary at A 136-8
client turning at A 141-5
conventional 95-6, 112, 246
development space of D 104-7
download and upload 83-4
for learning 83-4, 187
missed and intrinsic 194-6
moving for Clean Start 129-133
problem at B 97-100
process 33-4
self- 176, 183, 185, 261-271
space between of C 101-3,
150-152
the difference 85-6, 185, 272
timing of 43

Raj Joshi psychiatrist/online client
265-6
Randy Buckner psychologist 137
recording responses 138, 227
recursion 92
reflections 259-260
Reinforce (no. 3) 71-3
repetition 91-2, 226

Richard Bandler co-creator NLP 49
Richard Brenchley architect 9
Rob McGavock therapist 9, 53
witness client 251-2
Roloef Oldeman forest ecologist 9,
50, 84
Running the Numbers 245

Sandra weight loss client 95-9,
102, 174-5
scale of problem 123-4
selecting responses 227
Self Alignment process 273
self-facilitation 261-271
-healing 30
-reinforcing feedback 45
Seven the value 83-6
Shakespeare playwright 121
Sigmund Freud psychiatrist 8, 149
Silvie de Clerck creativity coach 9,
226, 243
Silvie double-bind client 105, 206-
216
Simon 'in a mess' client 176-187
Six as special 47-55
co-ordinates 82
degrees of freedom 167-221,
241
degrees of separation 49-51
first Grovian use of 49
Grovian history of 52-4
in structure of carbon atom 82
in structure of DNA 50, 82
in structure of universe 47, 84
-petalled *Agapanthus* 9
-Sided Table 256-8
sources of information and
redemption 49
-Space Symptom 237-241
stages of branching 50, 84,
214
-Step Brainwriting 48
-Step Reframe 49
the perfect number 81
the value 79-82
sixness 31-2, 228-9
sleep, importance of 165, 187

I know the ways of the sea
I know the winds and the currents
Fear not, and I will take you
to a larger and better land than this.

From the legendary voyage of Ru to Aotearoa

Printed in Great Britain
by Amazon

78120923R00163